EARLY PRAISE FOR
HOW TO SURVIVE SURVIVAL

"I remember the call that Saturday afternoon to go rescue an American citizen from Somalia. I remember tracking her health deterioration and austere living conditions narrowing our window of success. I remember helping our crews, team, and supporting personnel launch the aircraft to effect the rescue. I remember the day that American got a second chance at life. Jessica tells a story of turning adversity into strength. A story of never giving up. An amazing story of struggle and survival. And now, she wants to share the lessons she learned to thrive in life, be strong, and help others in the process. This book is the experiential account of a strong woman who defied odds in 2012, and that now wants to help others do the same. I am honored to be associated with Jessica, and proud of her accomplishments in life. You will not be disappointed!!!"

—SEAC (ret.) Ramon Colon-Lopez,
former Senior Enlisted Advisor to the Chairman
of the Joint Chief of Staff and Special Operations Pararescueman.

"Based on the opening pages, *How to Survive Survival* promises to be a powerful and compassionate guide for those navigating hardship and looking to reclaim meaning. Jess Buchanan's voice is steady and generous, and her message of transforming adversity into purpose resonates deeply. As someone who works closely with the Navy SEAL community, I see tremendous value in the strength and hope this book can offer."

—Robin King,
Chief Executive Officer, The Navy SEAL Foundation

"The raw reality of a life-altering event *can be* transformational. Jessica brings those realities and learnings to the reader through her real-life lived experiences. She brilliantly brings the reader into her mind, decisions, realities, and actions that have contributed to her successes as a spouse, parent, teacher, and global change agent. *How to Survive Survival*'s RISE framework is your playbook to a better version of you."

—Jacob Werksman,
DBA, Founder & CEO of Victory Strategies, Executive Fellow at Harvard Business School, and Former Navy SEAL

"This book is packed with wisdom learned through lived experience. Jessica speaks with total honesty about the impossibility of returning to the life lived before a trauma and addresses the difficulties the survivor and their families and friends face over the years, rather than months or weeks, when returning to an everyday and fulfilling life."

—John Smith,
Board Member and Cofounder, Hostage US; Former Chairman, Hostage International

"Jessica thoughtfully outlines the phases of survival, normalizing the complex emotions that often arise in the healing process. As a trauma therapist, I deeply appreciate the honesty and heart in this powerful book, which is not a quick-fix guide, but rather an authentic roadmap through the long, winding, and often painful journey of healing."

—Cindy Hanig, *LMSW*

HOW TO SURVIVE
SURVIVAL

OTHER WORKS BY JESSICA C. BUCHANAN

Impossible Odds:
The Kidnapping of Jessica Buchanan and Her Dramatic Rescue
by SEAL Team Six

Deserts to Mountaintops:
Our Collective Journey to (re)Claiming Our Voice

Deserts to Mountaintops:
Choosing Our Healing Through Radical Self-Acceptance

Deserts to Mountaintops:
The Pilgrimage of Motherhood

HOW TO SURVIVE
SURVIVAL

A Guide to Turning Life's Hardest Moments into Meaningful Contribution for the World

JESSICA C. BUCHANAN

Published and distributed by Soul Speak Press
An imprint of Merack Publishing

Library of Congress Control Number: 2025913765

Buchanan, Jessica C.
How to Survive Survival: A Guide to Turning Life's Hardest Moments into Meaningful Contribution for the World

Ebook: 978-1-958472-34-7
Paperback: 978-1-958472-35-4
Hardcover: 978-1-958472-36-1

This book was never meant to exist in isolation—because survival never happens alone. It is stitched together through community, courage, and connection. I am endlessly grateful to those who held me, challenged me, and carried this vision with me . . .

To my husband Erik—thank you for your love, your belief, and your willingness to share our story. You make everything feel possible.

To my children August and Ebba, who give me reason every day to keep going—you are the joy I fought to return to.

To my Dad and siblings Amy and Stephen, thank you for your unwavering love and continued wisdom and support.

To Aimee and Ryan—your friendship has been the foundation from which I could build a new life upon. Thank you.

To my fellow survivors, who trusted me with your truth—thank you for your raw honesty and your fierce hope. Your stories are the backbone of this book, and your willingness to speak out is a gift to the world.

To the Soul Speak Press team—Loren, Ilsa, Mieke, and every hand that touched this manuscript—thank you for stewarding this message with integrity, clarity, and heart.

To the readers who are holding this book in your hands—you are the reason this book exists. I hope it speaks to your ache, your resilience, and your longing to turn pain into purpose. You are not alone.

To SEAL Team Six, forever grateful doesn't cover it, but will have to do.

And to the version of me who once didn't know if she would make it: You did. And look what you've made from the wreckage.

CONTENTS

Foreword   1

Introduction   5

How to Use This Book   17

PART I: RECKON WITH THE PAIN   27

1   Okay, I Survived! Now What?   29

2   It Takes the Time It Needs to Take. No More.
    No Less.   43

3   Grief and the Mess It Makes   57

PART II: IDENTIFY THE IMPACT   71

4   Hindsight Gives and Takes Away   73

PART III: SEEK THE MEANING   99

5   The Alchemy of Meaning   101

6   Who We Become   117

7   The Great Invitation   131

8   Your Options, Your Choice   157

9   We Don't Rise Alone   167

PART IV: EMBODY THE PURPOSE   193

10 It's Okay to Want More Than Just Surviving   195

11 Healing Out Loud   211

12 Commit to Your Purpose   233

13 The Overflow   249

14 It's Time to Thrive   259

Conclusion   269

A Blessing for Your Next Chapter . . .   271

FOREWORD

I got to know Jessica Buchanan soon after I moved to Washington, DC, from London. It was five years after her rescue from captivity in Somalia by US Navy Seals, and she got in touch to see how she could help with Hostage US, the nonprofit I had relocated to the United States to stand up and run.

One day, she arrived at our office shaking. "Are you ok?" I asked, knowing the answer was no. Eventually, her breathing slowed, she was able to speak, and she told me she'd been overwhelmed by the lights and noise in the reception area. Five years on, the hypervigilance she developed as a hostage to stay alive was still there, holding back her recovery.

"It's so frustrating," she said. "No one tells you about the reality of surviving survival."

Surviving survival? I'd never heard that phrase. Jessica could see I was confused and intrigued. I leaned in. She told me that when you're a hostage you have to survive captivity. When you're released, your next job is surviving survival, building your life again, working out who you are and what your purpose is. And, she told me, staring intensely into my eyes, survival in many ways has a lot more to throw at you than captivity did.

1

At this point, I'd been supporting hostages and their families for over a decade. With colleagues in the UK, we had—brick by brick—built bespoke support services to help families get through the experience of having a loved one kidnapped, and to assist former hostages in getting back on their feet.

I was justified in considering myself something of a "hostage expert." *Surviving survival?* That was new to me.

The conversation with Jessica stuck. I had spent ten years working relentlessly to ensure hostages returning home would get the possible support they needed: health checkups, emergency dental work, physiotherapy, counseling, or financial assistance. There was no practical challenge too great. We spent three years going round in circles with the IRS until we finally found someone who agreed that, yes, the former hostage we were supporting should not incur late fees for the taxes he had failed to file while he was in captivity. Case finally closed.

I was proud of what we had built. Practical services create a stable foundation that allows a hostage's recovery to start.

They are a lifeline, for sure, but they are not what rebuilds your life force.

Once the dust has settled, the taxes have been filed, the physiotherapy completed, and the paperwork organized, what then for the human being who has survived a traumatic event?

The question Jessica poses in this book is beautiful in its simplicity: I survived, now what?

Now what?

Who am I? How and where do I find meaning? What makes me happy? What is my purpose?

Whether you were held hostage by Somali pirates, survived an abusive relationship, lost a child, or filed for bankruptcy, the answers to these questions offer the key to surviving survival. As Jessica says in the book, purpose is what creates resilience because it gives us something to fall back on when we inevitably falter. This book is an essential guide and companion for anyone wrestling with the messy and complicated road that follows trauma.

"So what happens when you've survived survival? What comes next?" I asked Jessica.

"Well, that's called thriving. And that's what I hope every former hostage can achieve."

Rachel Briggs OBE (Officer of the Order of the British Empire),
Former Executive of Hostage International and Hostage US
July 2025

INTRODUCTION

On October 25, 2011, I walked away from myself and through a doorway that led me into another life. I didn't know it then, but my intuition did, and it was screaming at me to listen. However, because of a low self-esteem and lack of self-awareness, coupled with the societal conditioning of keeping quiet that I had been subject to for most of my life, I was crippled in the face of my own decision making when the decision really mattered. Around three o'clock in the afternoon on that October day, I climbed into the back of a Land Cruiser that was sent to transport me and my Danish colleague from our office in the southern part of Galkayo, Somalia, to the northern part of the city. It was enroute to our office that my world came crashing down around me.

It started with another Land Cruiser roaring up along the right side of our vehicle and splashing mud up all over our windows and windshield. All I could think to say as I looked up from my phone and the email I was drafting was, "What a jerk! Who drives like that?" The butt of an AK-47 connecting with the hood of our vehicle told me all I needed to know. We were quickly surrounded by armed men who sounded incredibly angry, and I was afraid for my life.

It was just a few seconds before my greatest fear in life was substantiated: We were being kidnapped, driven deep into the desert by armed men, and I didn't know what they wanted. They demanded I hand over my passport, wallet, jewelry, work computer, and satellite phone—I obliged in hopes that it would appease my captors. But it was to no avail. What they wanted was me. Or rather, forty-five million dollars in exchange for me. I was the meal ticket for an entire crime ring, and a very vulnerable one at that.

Weeks turned into months. We were kept outside the entire time, driven from one place to another—just patches of desert where we settled under small groves of acacia trees. There was no shelter from the blazing African sun during the day, nor was there safety from the cold winds that would whip through the desert at night. I tried to sleep, surrounded by men and their guns. After a series of six proof-of-life calls, a proof-of-life video, and a urinary tract infection that was moving steadily into a kidney infection, unbeknownst to me, by order of President Barack Obama, on January 25, 2012, the elite SEAL Team Six parachuted into the desert, in the middle of the night, and successfully rescued me and my colleague.

It was life altering, not only the kidnapping, but the rescue. A more detailed account is available in my memoir, *Impossible Odds: The Kidnapping of Jessica Buchanan and Her Dramatic Rescue by SEAL Team Six.*

I cannot and probably will never be able to describe the feeling of liberation and freedom that came that night, after being held hostage for ninety-three days by armed pirates in the Somali desert. After being starved, tortured, abused, and kept just alive enough so that I could be cashed in, the fact that I survived that alone, was a miracle, and I, along with my entire family, was so grateful. But just like with anything in life, all good things must come to an end.

And that is when my next survival journey began.

In the months and years following my kidnapping experience, and my rescue by SEAL Team Six, my life changed in almost every single way a life can. Within the span of a month after my rescue, my husband and I found out we were expecting our first child. I was unable to return to my job with the international NGO I had been working for, and it became very apparent that I was no longer able to remain in Africa because my PTSD had become debilitating. After living in Kenya and Somalia for nearly a decade, my husband Erik and I had built a beautiful life we loved, doing work we really believed in, but the impact of my trauma had changed me so fundamentally that I no longer recognized myself, nor did I fit into this life I had so painstakingly created.

I've always found change to be incredibly exciting. I'm a fairly impulsive person (I'm sure that is no surprise based on my past experiences!) so the thought of relocating and starting over sounded like a wonderful adventure in the aftermath of so much darkness. I had no idea that my hardest days of survival were ahead of me, because living through the kidnapping had been fairly simple compared to what was to come.

With no solid place to land, or promise of employment, and just the social support of a few very good friends, on a cold March morning, my husband, my six-month-old son Auggie, and I landed at the Washington Dulles International Airport outside of DC with ten overstuffed suitcases and the clothes on our backs. We had sold everything we owned, packed a few beloved pieces of furniture into a shipping container, and left our two dogs behind so that Erik could return to collect them after we settled into our new home in the US. My dad lived in central Virginia at the time and so he offered to let us stay with him until we could figure out where we wanted to be. While I still view that time with him as incredibly special, it was challenging, isolating, and lonely. We went from a vibrant work and social life in Africa to quiet nights spent in the Blue Ridge Mountains with Grandpa, a baby, and—eventually—our dogs. It was only temporary, and I knew this, but still, my anxiety began to grow until I felt it was going to swallow me alive. There were very few distractions from our reality and nowhere to hide.

Fast forward several months, and we moved to Northern Virginia, a more urban environment. We began to make some friends, and started traveling to promote our *New York Times* bestseller. I thought the uptick in activity would take care of the mounting anxiety I felt at all hours of the day, but things just seemed to get worse for me, emotionally and mentally. I found a wonderful therapist and started seeing her once, sometimes twice, a week because I was in such a crisis. I don't know if I would be here without her. Thank God for therapists.

Maybe she told me this, and maybe I chose to ignore her. Maybe she didn't and I chose not to acknowledge what I knew deep down in my heart to be true: The reality was that I was "in it" for the long haul. This healing-from-trauma thing was deep, and it was going to take a while . . . if not the rest of my life to figure out who I was now as a result of the impact of the kidnapping.

Like many of you reading this most likely, I'm a type A personality, a get-it-done kinda girl. I go my own way, but if a path has been blazed already and I can see it will get me where I want to go more efficiently, I'll gladly take it! Working smarter, not harder, has always been foundational to my philosophy in life.

I quickly realized, much to my dismay, that there was no one path to healing, no checklist to consult. Everywhere I turned, it seemed what was being asked of me was patience, consistency, and . . . time. There was no hack. There were no shortcuts. There was just grueling hard work and waiting ahead.

Time did pass, sometimes painfully slowly, sometimes just painfully. In an effort to speed things up, I spent hours scouring the internet and asking my therapist the questions for which there seemed to be no answers. I would search for podcasts that could be helpful resources for my healing journey and spend money on books that just didn't quite hit the mark. I begged the Universe for *something* that would help speed up this healing process because I was in so much pain; I felt like I was being held hostage (and I do *not* use that term lightly!) to this trauma, and I desperately wanted to find a way to pay that ransom demand. *Isn't there anything out there that could help someone like me?* I wondered. *Isn't there a formula or a manual for healing that I could apply to my life to make me feel better?* In retrospect, I can see I was looking for a twelve-step program that would take me from broken-hearted to wholeness. I wanted something similar to those who experienced addiction and were seeking recovery. *Give me the steps to recover from the trauma of kidnapping! I'll do them all—I'm a wonderful student!* I would think. I tried all the things that people who are in recovery try: prayer, meditation, medication, green juices, yoga, therapy, herbal teas, journaling, energy healing, acupuncture. . . . And when those things didn't free me, I will be honest, I drank a lot of wine.

The truth is, there is no plan that maps out the exact steps to surviving survival. We've each been through something extraordinary, and what works for me might not work for you. Our traumas, our pain, while universal to the human experience, are not cookie-cutter and there are no exact steps to follow that will alleviate the crushing guilt of surviving the regret of making mistakes that result in life-changing consequences, or the struggle with a grief that you could never have imagined existing in your life. I have learned, over the years, a few tools and gained some insights that I do believe will help others, and that is why I have written this book. The advice often given to me, whether in business, or in search of purpose, has always been to create something that the past version of myself needed. That is our offering to the world. I couldn't find this when I needed it, and as I've moved through my healing experience, I have kept meticulous notes about what has worked for me and what has not. I am in no way declaring to have all the answers, or any, for that matter, but what I am trying to do is share my experience as I have, brick by brick, rebuilt a life I am proud of, a life I love.

I have also included stories from people who have done something similar. And while our circumstances are wildly different, our humanity and ability to survive trauma and its aftermath is something we have in common with each other, and with you, I suspect.

It is important for me to note that I am not a clinician of any kind, although I have had this manuscript reviewed and edited by a clinical therapist to ensure I have not simplified the impact that trauma has on us, or created a body of work filled with one-sided suggestions that only worked for me.

In my situation, the greatest gift I have been given is time. Time to reflect, space to ponder, the opportunity to grieve, and eventually to surrender to what is now and let go of what I once had. I've come to understand that there is no shortcut to healing, because things take the time they need to take. No more, no less. That has been one of the most crucial lessons I have learned in my lifetime. And I have my co-captive Poul to thank for that.

It took ninety-three days in captivity for me to learn that vital lesson. However, it would take me ten years of working through my trauma to understand just how much time healing actually takes and how much strength and practice resilience needs in order to be cultivated so it can grow into something beautiful. More than anything, I hope you will believe me when I say you can still make this life beautiful. All has not been lost, you have not been forsaken, and there is purpose in this chaos, even if you can't believe it right now.

And then, suddenly, without having realized it, there will come a point in your healing journey where you will have taken the time— you will have written everything there is to write about, you will have examined the pain and processed the most intricate parts with your therapist until your bank account is empty and you have cried all your tears and they finally stop taking you by surprise; and then, and only then, will you look in the mirror and ask this very different version of yourself staring back at you one of the most important questions of your life: I survived—*now what?*

After the searing pain of your tragedy has dulled to a less dramatic throb, you will begin to notice that you are really different now and the old life, the old friends, the old job, the old house, whatever it is that used to define you, pre-life shatter, just doesn't make sense anymore. Just like trying on my favorite pair of jeans a week after I had my first baby didn't fit the same, neither will the pre-trauma life fit this irrevocably changed version of you.

I remember my clarifying moment like it was yesterday. I was, indeed, standing in the bathroom after a long shower, staring into the mirror at a face that was still recognizable in many ways, but unfamiliar in others. I had been changed so fundamentally by my kidnapping experience, and it showed. My life was completely different, and I was caught at this perplexing point where I had no idea what to do with the rest of this life that had been so generously given back to me.

For so long, I had identified as a teacher who worked in Africa. I created that identity because it was what I wanted; it was how I wanted to be recognized. I took risks, made many good and bad decisions, and had the privilege of youth and the luxury of ignorance on my side back then. But with the kidnapping, the blinders had been lifted, and I had a whole lot of painful baggage I was now carrying into this next phase of my life. All I could think as I moved through my days at a snail's pace was, *now what?*

Part of this was complicated by early parenthood—having my first son less than a year after my rescue and his sister two years after that. I'm sure the now-what question is asked by many a mother who has locked herself in the bathroom to hide from her screaming toddlers! But my deep life contemplation was complicated by this significant trauma. While it took time (twelve years to be exact!), it also required brave exploration, experimentation, and the willingness to create a new life that was outside the box.

Now, I am writing what I so badly needed when I was up in the middle of the night soothing my daughter, my mind ruminating on the loop of what I was supposed to do next with my life. I often wondered on those dark nights, *if* there was anything left for me to do or become. I became so obsessed with this question that it gave me purpose for a while—this pursuit of resurrecting my "next thing." There were moments of gut-wrenching frustration and fear. I would often wonder, perhaps, if there was no *now what* left for me. I considered the possibility that my purpose had dried up in the desert along with my captor's hopes of collecting that forty-five-million-dollar ransom demand in exchange for my life.

* * *

I remember having dinner with a few friends around this time. I had grown close to these women, mostly because we were all experiencing a state of transition due to our unique circumstances. One of them must have grown tired of listening to me drone on and on about the now-what frustration I was experiencing in my life, and with a mild sense of exasperation proceeded to explain to me during dinner that there was no *now what* . . . she staunchly believed that there was no such thing as the "right thing" and that I was searching in vain for what I was supposed to do now.

My face flushed with embarrassment because I could see I had overstepped and gotten on everyone's nerves, but also because I felt so incredibly hopeless as I listened to her explain that there was no "thing." I wanted to fight back, give her the many reasons why my quest wasn't a totally useless and fruitless waste of time. But, I had nothing.

What I didn't understand then, and was unable to articulate that night at the table, is something I know now: My search for the next thing was really a pursuit of my purpose, and pursuing purpose is what defines our resilience as those who move from just surviving to *thriving*.

If there is anything I want you to understand as you read this book, it's that I believe deeply, in the most private part of my being, that nothing we go through in life is wasted. While often not of our choosing, our pain and tragedy have purpose and more significant meaning attached to them—but only if we let it be that way. You may be someone who doesn't believe that, and perhaps you would get along well with my friend from dinner! That is entirely okay and

I respect your opinion even if I wholeheartedly disagree! You might feel like throwing this book across the room because you think it's utter crap. After all, the pain you have experienced is so significant and extraordinary that you can hardly speak the words of what happened to you out loud. I want to say I am so very sorry for what you have been through. It's courageous of you to continue showing up in a life you could never have expected to feel such profound and inexplicable loss in.

That being said, it is no accident that you are here, nor do I believe you survived on an off chance or that it is some sort of mistake. You made it through the darkness and are standing here, blinking hard into the blinding light of your life. You may be a mangled, messy version of who you used to be, but you are still here—and, my friend, I believe, because I must, that it is very much on purpose.

Pain is an invitation to go somewhere deep inside us so that life can have its way with and in us. There is very little we can do to escape that reality. Many figure out a way to do it temporarily, but the truth will still come for you eventually. Purpose is relentless and the only way I have been able to heal my pain is to figure out how to do something meaningful with the lessons I have learned from my own survival, both during captivity and in the years that followed my rescue. There are several paths to choose from as you contemplate what moving forward might look like; I hope this book will be a guidebook to one of them for you.

You may still be in crisis, so please put this book down and save it for a later time when you have the strength to feel inspired and encouraged, if that is your reality right now. This book is not for you if you are still mourning or surviving trauma. But I do want to remind you, and maybe show you my heart as proof, that you will eventually emerge from the pain and numbness, and when you do, I hope you find this book on the back of your shelf when you finally get to the place in your existence where you are asking: *now what?*

And if you are on the edge of your bed, exhausted from your grief journey, yet you find yourself desperate for a new beginning, I am so glad you found your way here.

Take a deep breath, and let it out slowly.

The next chapter of your life is beginning and I promise you, it is going to be beautiful.

Not just for you, but for everyone in your world.

xx

HOW TO USE THIS BOOK

This book is not just something to read—it's something to *experience*.

The pages that follow are shaped around a framework I developed not just from research, but from lived experience—mine and the many survivors I've met along the way. It's called the **RISE Framework**, a four-part process designed to guide you from the raw aftermath of trauma into a life rebuilt with purpose, impact, and meaning.

RISE stands for:

- **R**eckon with the Pain
- **I**dentify the Impact
- **S**eek the Meaning
- **E**mbody the Purpose

Each section of this book corresponds with one of these phases. You'll find chapters that unpack the emotional, psychological, and spiritual terrain of each stage—not just through my own story, but through the stories of other courageous survivors. These "Survivor Spotlights" illuminate what it looks like to live each phase in real time: messy, nonlinear, deeply human.

The **RISE Framework** is not meant to be prescriptive. It's not a straight line. You might find yourself moving back and forth between phases—or living in all of them at once. That's normal. Healing doesn't follow a timeline. What this framework offers is *language* and *structure* for a process that often feels chaotic and disorienting. It gives you a way to name what's happening, and to trust that wherever you are, it is part of something larger.

Here's how to engage with it:

- If you're in deep pain or fresh grief, start in **Reckon with the Pain**. You'll find stories and tools that help you give voice to your heartbreak without rushing past it.

- If you're trying to make sense of who you are now, and how trauma has changed you, explore **Identify the Impact**. It will help you take inventory of what's shifted—internally and externally.

- If you're ready to search for meaning and direction, turn to **Seek the Meaning**. These chapters will invite you into reflection, curiosity, and maybe even glimpses of hope.

- And if you feel called to use your story to help others or contribute to something greater than yourself, **Embody the Purpose** will show you what it looks like to transform your pain into purpose.

I've woven this framework not only into the structure of each chapter but also into the storytelling itself—layered within personal reflections, survivor journeys, and thoughtful questions that invite you deeper into your own process.

This book is a conversation—a mirror, a guide, and a companion. It's an invitation to rise, at your own pace, in your own way.

At the end of each chapter, you'll find two key features to help you engage more personally with the material:

- **Pause, Ponder, and Process** prompts: These are reflective questions designed to help you deepen what you've just read and apply it to your own life. I highly suggest you bring a journal or computer with you when you read through these chapters so you can take the time to really dig in.

- **RISE Reminders**: These are short, powerful affirmations written in the first person, to anchor your healing and remind you of what's possible. I'm a big believer in affirmations (see what I did there!) and I write them all over everything. I have them on my desk, my computer, I program them into my phone on my alarm—I put them wherever I need to see them or just copy them over and over in order to make that brain-body connection. I encourage you to do what works for you!

This book is meant to meet you where you are—and gently guide you toward where you're going next. While this isn't a step-by-step manual, it *is* a guidebook. The margin notes, the white space, the questions—they're here for *you*.

And while it's entirely up to you how deeply you engage, I want you to know this: The prompts and reflections at the end of each chapter are where transformation really takes root. If you skip them, you may miss the richest parts of the journey.

So take your time. Go at your own pace. But don't be afraid to go deep.

I wrote this because I believe you're not here just to survive what happened to you.

You're here to live—and to live well. And I want you to receive everything this book has to give as you step into the next chapter of *your* story.

Introducing the RISE Framework: Reclaiming Purpose After Pain

The **RISE Framework** is named not only for the acronym, but also for what it represents: the rising we do after we've fallen, the meaning we begin to uncover when we are finally ready to look within and ask the deeper questions.

Each stage—**Reckon with the Pain, Identify the Impact, Seek the Meaning,** and **Embody the Purpose**—is rooted in real-life healing journeys, including mine. It's also backed by decades of psychological research on posttraumatic growth, meaning-making, and identity reconstruction after adversity. And most importantly, it's accessible. Whether you've faced trauma, loss, or any painful life disruption, this framework can guide you through the messy, sacred work of turning pain into purpose.

As you move through this chapter, I invite you to take your time. Don't rush the steps. Be honest with yourself. And remember: *This isn't about pretending the pain never happened. It's about making sure it didn't happen in vain.*

Let's walk through each stage together.

You've survived the unthinkable. You've mourned, you've grieved, you've spent time wondering how it all ended up so wrong and now you are ready, or perhaps, not ready, but your brain can at least wrap around the idea that there might be something worthwhile that can come out of this. Or, perhaps, all you really know is that you can't stay where you are for one more blessed day. Something needs to change but you don't know what and you don't know where to start. All you know is that you are here and there is something calling you to a new way of showing up because everything that you have spent building in your life is gone—or at least the person living that life is, and the one thing you do know is that you want to rise.

The RISE Framework: Reclaiming Purpose After Pain

R - Reckon with the Pain

Before you can rise, you must be willing to face what knocked you down. Reckoning means acknowledging the trauma, naming the loss, and letting yourself feel the grief. It's not about wallowing, but about witnessing. You can't heal what you won't name.

This is the part of the journey many people skip over, wanting instead to just "move on." Or, maybe the wallowing feels like the safest place for you right now, or perhaps the world around you is telling you it's time to get up and get your shit together. But healing doesn't work that way. As the saying goes, *you don't have to move on—you get to move forward*. And the only way forward is through.

It's messy. It's painful. It's hard. Which is why so many people won't do it. But you are here, so I'm guessing you are the kind of person who is curious about what this all could mean, not only for you and the ones you love, but for the world.

In their book *Open Up by Writing It Down*, authors and psychologists James Pennebaker and Joshua Smyth compile research showing that emotional processing—narrating your story, journaling, talking it through—activates parts of the brain associated with meaning and regulation, reducing the intensity of distress over time. In other words, telling the truth about your pain helps you metabolize it.

When I began reckoning with my own trauma, I had to revisit places in my memory that I had buried deep. I cried, I wrote, I shook. But I also started to feel something unfamiliar: relief. I was finally giving myself permission to feel what I had been running from: acceptance. And that changed everything.

I – Identify the Impact

After we face our pain, we begin to see how it shaped us. The second stage is about reflection—getting curious about how the trauma changed your beliefs, identity, relationships, and sense of safety. It's also the time to examine what stories you've started telling yourself about your worth, your role in what happened, and what your future looks like.

This is where we often find shame hiding in plain sight. It's where we confront the unconscious agreements we made in the dark like, "I'm not safe," or "It's my fault," or "I'll never be whole again."

Psychologists Richard Tedeschi and Lawrence Calhoun's 2004 research into posttraumatic growth has consistently shown that individuals who engage in reflective practices and cognitive processing report higher levels of growth in the domains of personal strength, spiritual development, and appreciation of life.

When I really took time to sit with the impact of my trauma, I discovered that I had been living in a constant state of deference—silencing my voice, deflecting my needs, and doubting my intuition. My healing began to accelerate when I named that pattern and began to rewire it. This step isn't about blame; it's about clarity.

S - Seek the Meaning

Now comes the sacred work of asking: *What is this pain here to teach me?* Not in a spiritual bypassing way, but in a grounded, courageous way that's willing to look for wisdom in the wreckage. Seeking meaning is about identifying what matters to you now. It's about locating the values that have endured—or emerged—since the pain. It's about asking your journal, your reflection, your best friend, and your therapist to help you figure out how you can rejoin the world with purpose and passion. Passion fades in the aftermath of chaos, and the hardest thing for me was the loss of my identity that was so deeply connected and rooted in my passion for helping kids in Africa.

You might discover that you're drawn to new causes, deeper relationships, or different priorities. Maybe it's your kids' health and recovery in the aftermath of a loss that you are now most passionate about. Maybe it is advocating for health reform after you have experienced a crisis in your own health journey. Whatever it is, you may find your sense of empathy has expanded, or that you now feel called to advocate, create, or support others in ways you never imagined.

Grief researchers Dr. Robert A. Neimeyer and Dr. Diana Sands have found that narrative reframing—viewing your story through a growth-oriented lens—has been shown to reduce symptoms of

PTSD and increase posttraumatic growth, especially when combined with guided reflection.

This is where my TEDx talk was born. I began to realize that "Change Is Our Proof of Life" wasn't just a speech title. It was a core truth I had lived and was ready to share. Meaning doesn't always show up in dramatic moments—it's often discovered in hindsight, through slow and honest reflection.

E - Embody the Purpose

The final stage is about movement. Taking what you've learned, what you've uncovered, and turning it into action. It's not about building a platform or starting a nonprofit (though you can). It's about small, aligned steps that reflect your renewed sense of self and service.

Purpose is not a destination—it's a direction. And meaning becomes real when you live it.

Recent studies by researchers Patrick L. Hill and Nicholas A. Turiano have shown that acting on a renewed sense of purpose leads to improved psychological resilience, greater life satisfaction, and even better physical health. Purpose is protective. It keeps us grounded. It gives the pain somewhere to go instead of eating us whole and swallowing us alive.

For some, this may look like mentorship. For others, creative work. For me, it meant telling my story, building a coaching practice and publishing company, and helping others mine the meaning in their own life stories. You don't have to have it all figured out and you don't have to do something grand. Maybe it's about deciding to be a friendlier version of yourself than you once were, or perhaps it's about how you show up for your kids. Whatever it is, you just have to be curious, willing to explore, and find a place to begin.

And as you do, celebrate. Let yourself feel the miracle of progress, the gift of your own evolution. Who you are becoming is a testimony—not just to what you've survived, but to what you've *chosen* in the aftermath.

If you're in the middle of a hard season right now, I want you to know this: You don't have to stay there. There is a way through. And the pain that's brought you here may just be the beginning of something sacred.

So let's not *just* walk it together. Let's **rise**.

PART I
RECKON WITH THE PAIN

CHAPTER 1
OKAY, I SURVIVED!
NOW WHAT?

Surviving: To remain, to continue to exist,
after the death of your life.[1]

It's a valid question. Perhaps one you are too embarrassed to say out loud or admit to anyone other than the morning pages in your journal. You've been through something so heartbreaking, so devastating, so completely life-altering, and it's left you in pieces; you aren't sure if you have the strength to pick yourself back up and put the shards of your shattered life back together. Or, maybe it hasn't been *that* earth-shattering of an ordeal (at least that's what you tell yourself anyway), and you're not sure your will to pick yourself back up is strong enough to continue living. Maybe, if you are honest with yourself, you're not sure if you want to survive. *Maybe*, you think,

1   *Oxford English Dictionary*, "surviving (n.)," June 2024, https://doi.org/10.1093/OED/1056538066.

it sounds better to just lay in bed and self-medicate so I can sink into oblivion until . . . until what? You fade away?

My dad generously offered to let me off the hook of living in the days immediately after the rescue. For a while all I could do was sit in the corner of the sofa and stare blankly, too tired and empty to engage in life as it was celebrating my rescue all around me. He sat down across from me with a cup of strong black coffee one morning and said quietly, "Jess, no one would blame you if you just decided to sit in the corner and stare at the wall for the rest of your life." Tears poured down my face because of all the people reading my mind and heart; it would be him. How could he know I was wrestling with that exact dilemma? It's not like I wanted that—I just wasn't sure if I had the strength or ability to do anything beyond just existing. It took some time, but somewhere, deep inside me, I was able to detect a little spark of something I knew to be true: I wanted more than to stare at the wall for the rest of my days. I had just done the desert equivalent of that for three months and it had not been fun. I held onto this deep belief that I had survived for a reason, and I felt the weight of responsibility to my family and my government to continue living a productive and meaningful life. I was just too tired, sad, and scared to figure out what it was right then.

There are many ways we respond to trauma, and I believe that we are all surviving something. We've either already survived it, we are surviving it right now, or we will survive it. I hate to break it to you, but no one escapes the human experience unscathed. If you really think about it, we are surviving "little-t traumas" regularly, most likely on a day-to-day basis.

It's the passive-aggressive coworker you've had to navigate (or figure out how to avoid) every day, the unacknowledged grief of losing a job, that fight with a family member, or perhaps the friend who never calls back anymore. Acknowledging the pain, instead of stuffing it down—even these seemingly little things—can keep us from buckling from the overwhelm of collective survival.

I won't judge you if you spend the rest of your days staring at the wall in the corner. You've been through some tough stuff, and I get it. But I am here to offer you my story and perhaps some ideas on why surviving survival is possible. My hope is that I can inspire you to turn your life's most challenging moments into meaningful contributions for others. My guess is that you came here looking for an alternative to staring at the wall and waiting for the end. Either way, it's no accident, and I'm incredibly grateful you are here.

Can I Survive Survival?

In the immediate hours, days, and weeks that followed my ninety-three-day captivity and successful rescue by SEAL Team Six, I was euphoric. Reuniting with my husband was as sweet and cinematic as I had visualized it would be as I wasted away in the desert. Hugging my father again and having dinner with my siblings was the healing balm my battered heart needed. Things I used to take for granted, like eating a salad or access to clean running water or sleeping in an actual bed, felt like a miraculous luxury. I remember leaping through the air while running next to the Zigzag River in an Oregonian forest, high on the intoxicating feeling of freedom. *I was alive! I was liberated! All was well!* But then, before I knew what was happening or could articulate what I was feeling, reality crashed all around me, and the euphoria evaporated into my memory like those SEALs that had parachuted into the night to rescue me.

* * *

The plummet began with two little pink lines at the end of a pregnancy test. Shockingly, I found out, just one month into freedom, that I was pregnant with my first child. Instead of reveling in my newfound freedom, I was hurling my stomach into the toilet bowl at all hours of the day and night. Flattened out by morning sickness that took hours, days, and months away from my new life caused depression and anxiety to take over what should have been an incredibly exciting time in our lives.

Lying in the darkness of my bedroom, tormented by nausea and nightmares, all I could think about was the horrific timing of everything and that I was going to be the most horrendous mother that ever gave birth to a child. My mother had suffered tremendously from depression after having my baby brother two decades earlier. I watched her fight hard for her sanity and, ultimately, her life. In and out of the psychiatric ward for years, her instability wreaked havoc on our family, and dealing with a similar fate was my worst nightmare, or one of them, at least. As I lay in bed, paralyzed by my fears, I pictured the same life I had experienced as a child playing out for my unborn baby. I heaved heavy sobs into my pillow as my husband stood by, watching helplessly. He had gotten his wife back, and yet he hadn't. It would take me many years to recover, heal, and figure out what all this meant for me and my new world.

In many ways, through many difficult days that followed, I felt guilty for thinking that surviving my life in the aftermath of my trauma often felt more difficult than surviving my actual kidnapping. When I sat down to consider the irony, I realized that surviving the kidnapping wasn't that tough because I only had one job to do: survive. But, surviving survival was a whole other ball of trauma that needed to be unraveled. And it wasn't one anyone had ever written a guidebook for, at least one that I could find. And believe me, I looked. I was bereft and lonely, grief-stricken, and sleep deprived. I had no idea what I was feeling, why I was feeling it, and if those feelings would ever go away. Therapists diagnosed me with complex post-traumatic stress disorder and prescribed Xanax to help keep the panic attacks at bay. They suggested that I do EMDR (Eye Movement Desensitization and Reprocessing) therapy, journal, meditate, and yoga. I did it all; I tried everything and was still anxious and listless. I traveled across the US to meet professionals who said they could "fix" me. Still, I suffered from debilitating panic attacks and felt a sense of dread every morning when I woke up and looked around me. I had everything I could ever want and had never been freer, and yet, I still felt held hostage to something unidentifiable and ominous. How can you solve a problem when you don't know what the problem actually is?

It was about four years into freedom when I finally realized what was "wrong" with me. Or at least I had a name for what I was experiencing. By happenstance (or, in my opinion, divine intervention) I came across a book by author and journalist Laurence Gonzales called *Surviving Survival: The Art and Science of Resilience.* Just the title stopped me in my tracks; I couldn't download the book fast enough on my phone as I headed out for my daily walk.

My walks were precious because they were my only time away from the kids (I had a three and one-year-old by now!), and I desperately needed to be a person and not a mother for forty-five minutes. I only made it partially through the first chapter when I had to stop on the sidewalk in my suburban DC neighborhood because I was crying so hard. *Finally.* Someone understood me. Finally, I had a name for what "this" was—this feeling that I didn't belong anywhere, that I didn't know who I was anymore because I had been changed so fundamentally by what had happened to me. The depression, the deep loneliness, the anxiety—they were all common experiences amongst those who had survived trauma like shipwrecks, shark attacks, or cancer—for those that had *survived survival*. I couldn't stop weeping and kept rewinding the chapter so I could listen to this particular excerpt again and again:

"Survival is one triumph, but living through that ordeal delivers us into the next stage of the journey. Adaptation means adjusting the self to a particular environment. If the environment changes, as it does through the experience of trauma, you are lost and must adapt once more. The bigger the trauma, the more dramatic the requirement for change. In many cases, the necessary adaptation is so extreme that an entirely new self emerges from the experience. In those cases, there is no easy return to the old environment. Sometimes you can't go home at all."

In just one paragraph, the author brought the past four years into focus, and everything seemed to make sense. Not only was I not the same girl who had gone on that work trip, only to be kidnapped and held hostage for ninety-three days, but I couldn't go home. Instead, I had been forced to start a new life in a new place, as a new person—all of which were unfamiliar to me.

No wonder I was struggling. I realized something very important, and I can't thank Mr. Gonzalez enough. Trauma changes us so fundamentally, that sometimes, we are a stranger even unto ourselves.

I took the next three days to devour the audiobook, and when I was finished, I realized I didn't feel so alone.

But I could also see I had some choices in front of me and a lot of work to do. Many people would hear "four years post-traumatic event" and consider that ample time for healing and recovery. I know my organization sure did, that was evident in the six months compensation I received for therapy—and that's it. But things take the time they need to take. No more. No less. And everyone's time-line for healing, recovery, and discovery is as unique to them as their experience.

What is Surviving Survival?

According to the *Merriam-Webster Dictionary*, the definition of the word survival is: "to manage or continue to exist, in spite of difficult circumstances."

Here's the thing: the difficult circumstances do not cease to exist once the traumatic event is considered over. They just change.

Just because you are not in immediate danger or your life isn't at risk anymore, or because any number of stressful and traumatic circumstances have eased up a bit, it doesn't mean your survival journey is over.

No one ever said this to me—not one therapist, that I remember, not the Department of Defense when I participated in their Hostage Reintegration Program, certainly not my organization. It would take me four years to find—on my own by accident (or Providence!)—Gonzales's work and learn the term *surviving survival* for me to understand that I was drowning in feelings of guilt and unworthiness, and that this period of recovery I was enduring was its own kind of survival journey.

Everyone expected me to be happy—at least, that was my interpretation. I had this beautiful, healthy baby boy, a memoir that hit the *New York Times* Best Sellers list, a substantial multi-city media and book tour, and then lucrative speaking invitations to follow. I had a significant book advance and the freedom to travel worldwide with my husband and child. I had respect and admiration; even the

President of the United States knew who I was and invited me to attend the State of the Union address.

But, despite all of that, I felt like I was dying. And I felt so damn guilty about it. Here I was, with this life that had been given back to me, and it was gloriously beautiful, but sometimes, and I could barely even admit this to myself, I longed for the days of captivity because it was all so . . . simple. While I was out there in the desert, I had only one job to do. It was simply to survive. It didn't matter what I wanted or who I was—there were no decisions to be made, there were few choices to contemplate. I got up off my mat in the morning as the sun came up, moved my mat to the tree where I would sit for the next twelve hours. Kept my eyes on the ground when approached by my captors, said nothing, and just tried to live through another day. Compared to life outside, in freedom, that felt easy, controllable, and almost safe. It's weird, I know, but it's a common experience for many kidnapping survivors, especially, but I've talked with a few special forces veterans who have said similar things about being in combat.

I carried around this enormous guilt for not being happier with my life and my freedom. I was grateful, yes, but I was also miserable. I didn't know then that we can hold two opposing emotions simultaneously and that both things can be true at the same time. The aftereffects of losing my job, moving away from my home of ten years, starting over in a completely new environment, in a new life stage, and a new life role (motherhood is disorienting enough, without adding all the PTSD on top of it) were brutal. I was in tremendous emotional pain and had no idea who I was now or what I wanted, let alone any ability to figure out how to formulate a plan for what to do about any of it.

I remain convinced that God sent me straight into mother-hood to keep me from languishing in the bottom of a bottle of white wine every night. I would have checked out, and the truth is, I could have still, but somewhere deep inside me knew, in the wee hours of all those early mornings when I would get up, *again*, to nurse my son and rock him back to sleep, that I had it in me to show up and survive whatever this was I was going through. I had survived circumstances far more challenging than this. And I decided at some point that I was going to do whatever it took to survive my survival, because I wanted to be resilient.

I've spent years advocating, mainly within the former hostage and detainee world through my volunteer work with the DC-based nonprofit Hostage US, about this space in time that we refer to as *surviving survival*. However, this doesn't just apply to hostages. This recovery period affects any human in the aftermath of their survival story. Divorce, disease, bankruptcy—you can fill in the blank.

In his book, Gonzalez writes, "Your experience of life in the aftermath may be even more dramatic, and sometimes more painful, than the experience of survival itself. But it can be beautiful and fulfill-ing too, and a more lasting achievement than the survival that began it all. What comes after survival is, after all, the rest of your life."

Gonzales is accurate in his statement—life has the potential to be beautiful and fulfilling after survival, yet we can't ignore the fact that surviving survival is difficult because there are so many options, even too many options. And when we have too many options, we feel out of control, which is entirely counterintuitive. Perhaps having a lot of options on any old regular day feels like a gift to most peo-ple—but to the trauma survivor, it is paralyzing, panic-inducing, and a heavy responsibility that our brain convinces us will send us right back to our version of captivity if we make the wrong choice. This is why surviving the event wasn't so hard. There were few choices to make—mostly the choice was just to survive, and most of us want to survive.

While I feel like there is more conversation about this particular part of our healing journey in the contemporary zeitgeist of mental health, certainly more than there was ten years ago, I still feel like this explanation and how to deal with it is missing from the general trauma recovery toolbox. And while I cannot call myself a clinician or a scholar in areas of mental health, I can still remember how it felt to be so desperate for help, guidance, and tools to move me through—and support me and show me the way out of—that dark forest of survival to finally be able to step into the light of freedom. Even my therapists and trauma counselors didn't know what to say. It's taken me a decade to get to the other side of that forest, but I am now standing in my own light, ready to shine in order to light the path for others.

I hope that the following chapters will offer you solace, support, and guidance, as well as inspiration and hope. Not only will I be sharing my own stories to illustrate the tools I have used to heal and find my purpose, I will be sharing other inspirational journeys of women and men who have turned their horror into contributions for more than just their world.

There is a purpose and a plan for your pain, my dear friend. Surviving survival is an invitation to step into the possibility that there is a greater purpose for all the pain you have been through and somehow have figured out how to survive. If it feels like a big and overwhelming place to be in, that's okay because the truth is, it is. You've got a lot of choices in front of you. Hopefully, I can make the case for not only surviving survival, but thriving too.

Surviving Survival Starts with Reflection . . .

Take a moment to reflect on your journey and any insights you've gained through this process. Remember that healing and transformation take time, and every step forward is a victory. You are strong, and your survival story has meaning. These questions are designed to help you process your journey, reflect on your survival, and explore how you can turn your experience into growth and contribution. Take your time with each question, allowing yourself to be honest and open.

"Surviving is just the beginning.
What you do with it is what shapes your life."

PAUSE, PONDER, AND PROCESS

1. **What was the hardest part of your experience, and how did you overcome it?**
   Write about the most challenging moments and the ways you managed to get through them.

2. **What emotions are you still carrying from that time?**
   Identify any lingering emotions—fear, anger, grief, gratitude—and reflect on how they show up in your life today.

3. **What personal strengths did you discover in yourself during survival?**
   List the qualities and strengths you didn't realize you had before this experience.

4. **How has your perspective on life changed since going through this challenge?**
    Describe any shifts in your values, priorities, or outlook on life.

5. **What moments of resilience are you most proud of?**
    Celebrate your victories, no matter how small

6. **What aspects of your past survival still affect you today?**
    Consider triggers, habits, or thoughts that stem from your experience.

7. **What self-care or healing practices help you move forward?**
    List things that bring you peace, whether it's therapy, art, movement, meditation, or something else.

8. **What negative beliefs did you develop from your hardship, and how can you reframe them?**

9. **How do you define success and happiness now compared to before?**

10. **What new opportunities or personal growth have emerged from your struggles?**

RISE Reminders for Your Second Survival
R – Reckon with the Pain

- I'm allowed to admit that survival came with a cost.
- I can tell the truth about what hurt me—even if I don't fully understand it yet.
- Just because I made it through doesn't mean I'm "fine."
- I survived something hard. It's okay if I'm still unraveling it.
- I won't shame myself for how long healing takes.

I – Identify the Impact

- I am learning to name what's still hurting and what's still healing.
- My story reshaped me—and I'm allowed to figure out who I am now.
- I can feel both grateful and overwhelmed at the same time.
- I am not weak for still struggling. I am human.
- Just because I don't feel like myself doesn't mean I've lost myself.

S – Seek the Meaning

- I don't need to have it all figured out to begin again.
- The fact that I'm asking "What now?" is a sign of strength.
- There might be meaning here—but I get to look for it in my own time.
- I don't have to go back to who I was. I can become someone new.
- I'm allowed to believe there's something more for me, even if I don't see it yet.

E – Embody the Purpose

- Surviving was the first act. What comes next is mine to create.
- I am still here—and that matters.
- My pain has weight, but so does my presence.
- Even the smallest steps forward are worth honoring.
- I don't need to have all the answers—I just need to keep choosing life.

CHAPTER 2

IT TAKES THE TIME IT NEEDS TO TAKE. NO MORE. NO LESS.

Enough time had passed in captivity that Poul, my co-captive, had grown out his hair and a full beard so that he resembled a smaller Danish version of Willie Nelson. He had asked for a scrap of fabric from my headscarf to wrap around his forehead to keep the sweat from dripping into his eyes. As I watched him sit still in the middle of the mat, I paced in panic; I couldn't discern whether I was angrier at him for getting us into this situation in the first place or myself, for not listening to my intuition when I had known something bad was going to happen. We were both filthy and in need of medical care, and as I paced across our eight-by-six-foot mat, I glanced over at Poul in his seemingly monk-like posture, arms wrapped around his knees, gaze fixed peacefully on some focal point further off in the desert.

Whipping around to block his view, anger blazed in my belly and erupted out of me hot as fire as I shouted into his zenned-out face, "How long is this thing going to take?!?!?"

It wasn't the first time I had shouted this unanswerable question in exasperation up into the Heavens, but on this morning I was at the end of my rope, and all my anger was focused on Poul. Days had turned to weeks and weeks had crawled into months. I had contracted a urinary tract infection at this point, and I was worried that if it continued to go untreated, I was going to find myself in real trouble soon.

I threw my hands up into the air and then covered my face in despair. As I crumbled to the ground and took the same posture as Poul, I couldn't believe how easy it was to wrap my arms around my now too-thin legs. I looked over to Poul for any reaction, but he continued staring unblinkingly out into the open expanse of the Somali sky. I began to weep silently at first, and then my silence gave way to sobs, racking my skinny frame with actual force. As I wiped the snot from my nose with the end of my headscarf, I saw Poul stare at me from the corner of my burning eyes.

I turned to face him, waiting for him to say something that would make me feel hopeful.

Looking back out over the desert, he did say something; and while I didn't know it then, it would change how I experienced the human condition for the rest of my life.

"Jessica," he said, emphasizing the "Jess" because of his Scandinavian accent. "It will take the time it needs to take. No more, no less."

Fresh tears fell onto my torn and filthy *dirac* as I processed his words and looked out over the desert landscape. I decided very quickly that I hated them, and hated him, for saying them. But even then, in the middle of this horrible situation, I knew no truer words had ever been spoken.

Things were simply going to take the time they needed to take. There was nothing we could do to speed them up or slow this thing down because we simply were not in control.

My heart broke.

And then after some time, I made the choice to surrender.

To time. To God. To life.

No more than I had to, and fortunately, no less.

* * *

It was a gradual progression, but all throughout the captivity, and then especially after we were freed, "It takes the time it needs to take" became my mantra on the days that felt like I was making zero progress in my emotional recovery. I had promised myself that no matter how much time I spent as a hostage, when I got out, my priority would be the recovery of my mental health and seeking out emotional support. However, a wrench got thrown into my mental health support plan when I found out I was pregnant. As quickly as those two pink lines appeared on the pregnancy test stick, my plans to prioritize my healing flew out the window.

Yes, I went to therapy once, sometimes even twice, a week.

Yes, I explored other highly recommended trauma treatment modalities that offered brief respites of relief.

Yes, I took medication for my PTSD and postpartum anxiety.

But, I realized after a short time, just like during captivity, I was in this for the long haul. I had to be committed, no matter how much time it was going to take because now, I had a baby boy who was depending on me to be the best version of myself.

I began noticing that nothing I took, read, watched, or moved to, not even meeting with my therapist every day, could take the place of the healing power of *time*. There was no formula or short-cut—there was no hack. I was going to have to wait it out, commit to the work of my recovery, and figure out how to survive with patience, grace, and self-compassion. It was as gut-wrenching of a realization as understanding I had become a hostage.

It was another event in my life that could only be handled through the difficult choice to surrender.

Renowned physician Gabor Maté, who specializes in the link between trauma and autoimmune conditions, as well as neurodivergence, has written that "all of Western medicine is built on getting rid of pain, which is not the same as healing. Healing is the capacity to hold pain." What a mind blowing concept for a culture who is obsessed with escaping discomfort through various methods of scrolling, shopping, consuming, and numbing out.

Just like the age-old adage of building muscle strength at the gym, learning a new language, creating an artful masterpiece, or building a successful business takes everyone a different amount of time, and so does our emotional healing experience. It must be built on a foundation of possibility to allow our pain to be placed in a strong enough receptacle to hold it. Those possibilities can only be identified after we enable the immediacy of our trauma to settle down, allowing ourselves to retreat from the world, rest often without guilt, repair our relationship with our internal voice, and then take on the responsibility needed to rebuild our lives in a way that does not glorify nor compromise our resilient nature.

It is so utterly counterculture to the instant-gratification, social media-obsessed society we live in today, it's hard to understand that a key tool for healing after surviving is *time*; time to work through, live in, and process the pain. We understand that our actual trauma event may have been fast although furious, and yet no one notifies us that something painful that occurred in five minutes or five days can take years to emerge from. Healing is slow and achingly insignificant in its timeline. The world around us gets so impatient with the actual time we need to take to heal enough so that we can hold the pain. We are constantly interrupted in our recovery with the demands for productivity, which means many of us never truly get the chance to focus on our healing journey, so we walk around with an emotional limp or fighting a rising panic as we fail at getting answers and treatment for our autoimmune disease or declining mental health. We overcompensate with humor that deflects off walls we have resurrected to keep our battered little hearts safe. Often, we numb out by drinking, eating, shopping, or, in some cases, by overachieving. As time passes we find ourselves drifting deeper and deeper into the sea of sadness, confused, directionless, and void of hope or possibility.

Dr. James Doty, professor of neurosurgery at Stanford University, where he also serves as the founding director of the Center for Compassion and Altruism Research and Education (CCARE), explains his theory in his interview with the uber-popular thought leader and podcaster Mel Robbins that people who have experienced pain often take one of two tracks as time ticks on—the first one leads off into that sea I just described and is usually fraught with alcohol and drug abuse, leading to serious mental health and substance abuse issues. Then there are the overachievers who take the second track and will produce two opposing mindsets. The first set of overachievers believe they got to where they are through their own sheer will and determination, and so stay in that space and refuse to offer help to anyone else because "I got here alone, and I don't owe anyone anything!" The second set of overachievers understand pain and suffering on a cellular level; as a result, they want to help others find relief the same way they have. They believe their pain can be used as a resource for someone else's possibility.

While I can't really contend with a neurosurgeon from Stanford, I was recently chatting with a therapist friend of mine who offered a different take. She reminded me that pain is rarely linear, and it's almost never confined to just two or three tracks. It's more like a vast and tangled web—layered, looping, and unpredictable. Some days we grieve. Other days we rage. Some days we create, contribute, and shine. And some days, we just get by.

There's no universal roadmap for surviving survival. And while models like Dr. Doty's offer helpful insight, they can't capture the wild, nonlinear, deeply personal terrain of healing that each of us must walk.

No one has been in your shoes—they have never walked the survival story you have walked—and so they don't get any say in what's hard for you, how long it takes before it doesn't feel too hard, or what you do or don't want to do in the aftermath. Understanding and embracing that truth is freedom. At least it was for me.

One thing I've come to understand and accept is that my healing journey will never be done. And I'm okay with that. Because I have to be. Because healing, for me, isn't about completion. It's about continuing.

Survivor Spotlight: Erica Kenny—When Healing Takes Its Time

Some stories don't begin with a decision, they begin with space; and sometimes, it takes decades before that space arrives.

When I met Erica Kenny, I knew her as a gentle, thoughtful mother at the international school in Nairobi, where I was teaching her son's fourth-grade class. She was soft-spoken, kind, and deeply observant—an introvert who seemed to carry something quiet and holy beneath the surface. At the time, I had no idea what she had survived.

A few years earlier, Erica had come to Kenya with her husband Aaron, and their two young children, as missionaries from Canada. Their work focused on serving Somali refugees in Eastleigh, one of Nairobi's largest urban settlements. But while she came to serve a community far from home, she also began to confront something much closer to her heart: the trauma she had carried, silently, since she was a child.

Erica had grown up in a deeply abusive home; her father was both physically violent and sexually abusive. Although he was a devout member of their Catholic church, and even respected by others, Erica and her sisters lived a far more terrifying reality behind closed doors, and no one outside the family knew what was happening.

Erica had learned early to survive by staying silent, by shrinking, by believing the lie that she didn't matter. Only her husband Aaron knew the truth and so he protected her unwaveringly. She spent the early years in their marriage really staying in the shadows of his pastoral position. She homeschooled their children and didn't get overly involved in the Canadian Baptist church they were charged with.

When Erica was asked to join a short-term mission trip to Kenya with members from their congregation, she laughed. There was no way she could do something like that without Aaron going with her, or so she thought. He encouraged her to go, and after some cajoling, she agreed.

She went, unsure and scared. And when she returned to Canada, she was certain of one thing: *I'm never doing that again.* The pain, poverty, and intensity of what she had seen in Nairobi overwhelmed her sensitive, empathetic heart and she knew she just couldn't take it again.

But one year later, they moved to Kenya full time, and that's when something unexpected began to shift.

In the midst of their work with Somali women—many of whom had also survived violence—Erica began to see herself differently. As she connected with the women who started trusting her and telling her their stories, she didn't feel quite so invisible anymore. She started considering that perhaps she wasn't a weak person with nothing to say, but maybe she was someone who was meant to make a difference in the lives of these women. Maybe, she really and truly did have something to offer. Could it be that her story didn't have to end in silence, but rather, it could be a tool to connect with other women and help them understand they were not alone?

"I had always believed I was quiet and insecure because of what had happened to me," she said. "But now I understand I have a voice. And I have a right to use it. In fact, I have a responsibility to use it."

Being far from home, away from the systems and shadows that had kept her quiet, gave her something she had never had before: space.

Room to ask: *What happened to me?* And the freedom to say: *It wasn't my fault* and that's when the healing began—not in a rush, not in a single moment, but in slow, sacred layers. Because healing takes the time it needs to take and doesn't start until it knows you are ready.

Erica began working with a therapist and then began processing the grief she had buried for so many years. As a result, she began to believe, for the first time in her adult life, that she mattered.

About four months into their mission, she met a newborn baby girl who had been abandoned in a tea field and left for dead. She had been delivered to an orphanage called The Nest and her temporary name was Baby Hope. She was malnourished and her skin was completely melting off and she screamed—for four years straight. They came to find out she had been going through withdrawal when she was born, and it would take two long, bureaucratic years to adopt her.

Finally, Hope became Ava, Erica's daughter, and over time, she understood why they had been led to Kenya: Ava was the final piece in a family that had fought hard to find one another.

Erica doesn't pretend that this healed everything, and what I love most about her is that she doesn't subscribe to tidy answers like "everything happens for a reason." She is open about the fact that she was angry with God for a long time, and that she struggled with questions like, *Why didn't You stop it?* and *Why did I have to suffer?*

What she believes now is quieter, but more powerful: Her truth is that God didn't cause her pain, and He never abandoned her in it. He was there, even when she didn't know it.

It took over twenty years for Erica to begin facing what had happened to her, and another five before she started to speak about it. But healing doesn't work on our timeline; it comes when it's ready and when we're safe enough to start doing the hard work of leaning into the pain. Sometimes, it's only when we're far enough from the places that broke us that we are able to finally look back and say: *That wasn't my fault. I didn't deserve that. I am allowed to heal.*

Now, Erica uses her story to help others find the courage to speak, through her writing and the grief groups she runs, she shares with others that they don't have to carry their own silent wounds.

"I hurt for other people," she says. "And I want to use my voice to help them."

That voice, once silenced by violence and shame, now carries truth, tenderness, and strength.

Because some healing takes time, and some voices take time to find.

But when they do, they ring like freedom.

How Erica's Story Reflects the RISE Framework

Erica's journey is a sacred reminder that healing does not arrive on command. It unfolds—slowly, quietly, and in its own time. Her story shows us that sometimes surviving survival means giving yourself the space to grow, grieve, and reclaim what was never yours to carry in the first place.

R – Reckon with the Pain

For over twenty years, Erica carried the trauma of her abuse in silence. It wasn't safe to speak. It wasn't time. When she finally had enough distance—from her abuser, from the systems that kept her quiet—she began the courageous work of facing her pain head-on, but she didn't rush it. She allowed it to surface when it was ready, and in doing so, she gave herself the dignity of truth.

I – Identify the Impact

Erica had long believed that her quietness, her insecurity, and her sense of invisibility were just who she was, but as she began to heal, she realized they were the scars of what had happened to her. She started to see herself clearly—not as broken, but as someone who had survived something brutal and was still choosing to love, to serve, and to show up.

S – Seek the Meaning

Meaning came in layers. It came in her work with Somali women who had their own unspoken grief, and it came through her daughter Ava, whose life intersected with hers in a way no one could have planned. Meaning came through the realization that God had not caused her pain—and had never left her in it. Erica's healing wasn't found in answers, but in presence and purpose and in the knowing that her voice could now make others feel less alone.

E – Embody the Purpose

Today, Erica is using her story—not to explain her past, but to illuminate the path for others. Whether she is reading scripture from the pulpit or leading a grief group, she reminds people that silence is not the end. Erica models what it means to survive survival—not through volume, but through depth, and in doing so, she extends a legacy not of trauma, but of tenderness, truth, and transformation.

PAUSE, PONDER, AND PROCESS

1. **What does healing mean to you?**
   Write about what healing looks and feels like to you right now, knowing this definition may evolve.

2. **What expectations do you have about your healing journey? Are they realistic?**
   Examine any pressure you may be placing on yourself to get better in a certain way or time frame.

3. **How have you already grown, even if you don't always recognize it?**
   List small victories, mindset shifts, or ways you are different from when you started this journey.

4. **What does it feel like when you take two steps forward and one step back?**
   Acknowledge the frustration of setbacks, and explore how you can be kinder to yourself when they happen.

5. **What are some things you can remind yourself of when you feel like you are "failing" at healing?**
   Write affirmations or comforting words to revisit in tough moments.

6. **What are some signs that you are healing, even if they seem small?**
   List any changes in your thoughts, emotions, or actions that indicate progress.

7. **What emotions or patterns seem to repeat themselves in your healing process?**
   Recognize cycles in your emotions, triggers, or setbacks without judgment.

8. **What helps you when you feel stuck in your healing?**
   Explore tools, people, or practices that support you when progress feels slow.

9. **How can you practice self-compassion when you feel like you should be "further along"?**
   List self-kindness strategies for moments of doubt.

10. **How do you know when you need to rest versus when you need to push yourself gently forward?**
    Reflect on the balance between giving yourself grace and challenging yourself to keep growing.

RISE Reminders

- I don't have to rush my healing to prove I'm strong.
- I can't heal in environments that hurt me. It's okay to create space.
- I trust that what's unfolding in me will make sense in time.
- I trust that healing is happening—even when it feels still, or quiet, or far away.
- I don't have to be fully healed to be deeply helpful.
- My healing is its own offering—and it's unfolding exactly as it should.

CHAPTER 3
GRIEF AND THE MESS IT MAKES

I didn't know it was possible to grieve something other than the loss of a person, a pet, or perhaps a relationship, before the kidnapping. I knew of sadness, anger, and anxiety—we were very well acquainted, indeed. But up to about one year before the kidnapping, I had escaped the human experience of grief, for the most part. When my mother died suddenly, six days after her fifty-seventh birthday, fourteen months before captivity, grief steamrolled my naivety and shattered me.

I had experienced hardship, trauma, and abuse at different times in my life. But none of those experiences could have ever prepared me for the paralyzing hold grief had on my mind and spirit in those early days of the loss of my mother. I reached for the tools I knew might help ease my deep pain—yoga, prayer, quiet, and, sometimes, red wine. I remember many evenings, after I returned to work in Somalia after her funeral, where I would just lie on my yoga mat in the semi-darkness, paralyzed by the heavy weight of my emotions.

Instead of moving through a flow series, I could only fold into the fetal position on the floor and sob until the sun went all the way down. I spent hours alone in the dark with only my grief and the memories of my dead mother to keep me company.

That grief had to be put on hold when I was taken. There was no room to continue processing the loss for me or my family because our reality demanded we deal with the unpredictability of such an extraordinary life-and-death situation. I've never been great at compartmentalizing, but this was a matter of sheer survival. I also felt my mother so close to me during those ninety-three days. Her energy, spirit, whatever you want to call it, was so clearly present in the darkest moments of my captivity, and that enabled me to put my grief in storage somewhere within the caverns of my heart. I made a commitment to myself, even while being held, that when I got out, I would deal with the grief. I was not going to stuff it down and ignore it. I had learned the hard way that what gets stuffed down will always find a way to come back up—and usually with force. It is the physics of the heart.

Fast forward a little over a year later, and my husband and I decided to leave Kenya in pursuit of support and healing for my trauma; I honestly thought we would return to Africa quickly. In my mind, I thought we were taking a break to rest, restore, and heal, and then we'd be able to come back to Africa and resume life as we had always known it. I look back on that time and chuckle—boy, was I cute!

As soon as we landed in the US, I wanted to leave. I was utterly overwhelmed with the transience of our situation. I had no idea where to go, how to fit in, and if I would ever belong. My grass-is-greener survival trait kicked in with a vengeance, and the more complicated things felt in my new life, the harder I begged my husband to take me back to Africa. I would plead through my sobs for him to take me "home." I felt almost like I was being held hostage to this conventional life I had not chosen. While compassionate, Erik was firm in his belief that I wasn't ready to go back to Africa and that we needed to give building a new life here in the US a chance. I was having none of it, and as a result, it made both our lives miserable.

This was the beginning of a heartache I had never known was even possible. I had had my heart broken before, shattered into a million pieces by abuse and deception. I think, primarily because I was young and relatively carefree, I was able to piece my life back together over a short amount of time. I had youth, freedom, and adventure on my side. The older I got, the more responsibilities I acquired, and as my attention was pulled in different directions, the ability to identify my pain and direct time and focus on healing was slow and often misplaced.

I remember being unable to even look at my Facebook friends' posts who remained in Africa shortly after we moved back to the States—the pain I felt when watching their lives play out online was the same way someone would feel when watching their ex gallivant across social media with a new love. It was a crippling, indescribable pain that I couldn't articulate because I was unable to connect my feelings with the loss of one person, per se, or even really the loss of a particular thing. The sadness was inescapable, though, and the harder I tried to run from it, the more it became a part of me.

It took me many therapy sessions, multiple journals filled, and yes, so much *time* to understand that what I was feeling was grief, and not just of one thing, but of all the things. I was grieving the loss of not just an entire life that I had so painstakingly built, but I was also grief-stricken over the loss of my sense of self, which was intricately connected to my work in Africa. I had derived my identity from this self-proclaimed purpose, and without either of them, I had no idea who I was or how to be in the world. Truth be told, I'm embarrassed now about how much of my identity and purpose were intertwined with my work in Somalia. In *Impossible Odds*, I write about how my college friends and acquaintances called me "Africa Jess." It took me many years to understand that Africa had never invited me to come in and do the work. I had taken that upon myself, and the identity I had created for myself inside it was a construct that I had built out of good intentions but had not considered the impact.

One of the hardest things grief can do is strip us of our identity, not the outside appearance, but rather, hollowing us out, leaving this enormous hole where the wholeness of us, our essence used to reside. Confusion, anxiety, and directionlessness can quickly take the place of our essence, which is what we would consider our North Star.

While I was steeped in my grief over having left the home I loved so much, and consequently, leaving my identity and my purpose behind, I found brief respite from my agony during my daily walks. After I dropped my kids off for their morning preschool activities most mornings, I would walk a three-and-a-half-mile loop around my neighborhood, hoping to clear my mind and heart before I would tend to little people for the rest of the day. I probably walked this route thirty times before I noticed an old, half-rotten, hollowed-out tree rooted into the edge of the woods one morning in the early spring. Crocuses braved their way to the surface of the soil, warming their little lavender faces in the cold spring sun. As I stopped and surveyed this rotting tree, I felt compelled to walk closer; I needed to inspect it. The closer I came, the more I could see that while the top of the tree was gone due to decay, surprisingly, its trunk was thriving with life that had taken up residence inside it. Along the interior of its hollows, bright green moss grew, offering all sorts of critters shelter, comfort, and hydration. Mushrooms were popping up off to the side, extracting the tree's medicine as it no longer needed to provide nutrition for its roots; I was intrigued at how, even in such a state of dilapidation, it could still offer life to another thing. As I approached, a squirrel popped out of the top, surprising us both. I chuckled, having jumped five feet in the air on account of the sweet rodent who scurried past me, settling in the branches of another nearby tree to watch from a safer distance. As I observed the wood and all the life growing within it, I knew the Universe wanted to teach me a lesson. Here I was, feeling as hollowed out inside as this dead tree, my roots having been pulled up quite violently, then dropping me in a place I didn't know if I had the strength to thrive in. I felt a kinship with this piece of nature, like we were both standing there, worn out and ready to take a long deep sigh before we moved on to what was next.

As I stroked the damp wood with my hand, I was struck with the realization that even though the tree's original purpose was no longer relevant, it was not altogether purposeless in its existence. Even though the top had fallen, and it no longer used its life force to shoot buds and green leaves up into the sky, it still served an essential purpose within the forest's ecosystem. Its hollows, once solid and strong, had been converted into shelters for birds, bugs, and rodents, keeping them safe from the elements. The bark had become food for growing fungi, and in that moment, as I continued to contemplate the purpose of this tree, I received a beautiful lesson about grief: Yes, it was true that one life purpose was over and done with for this tree, but just because it wasn't doing what trees were supposed to do anymore, that didn't mean another purpose wasn't possible, and a new life couldn't begin—one in which it could be of benefit and contribution to the world around it. It would look different, yes, but the purpose of the tree was meaningful and just as important as when it had been standing tall, waving its long branches in the summer sun.

I still walk this route, even though my children are long past their preschool years. And I will stop my stride when I get to this tree and say hello. She is not as lively a hub for the wildlife she once was, but against all odds, she still remains standing, able to take on the brunt of the wind, rain, snow, and whatever else Mother Nature throws at her. Over time, the tree has evolved to match the changes that have been forced upon her by the environment all around. I like to think this tree, if it had been given a choice between a final end or being of service to the world around her, was able to move through her grief of not being a lively tree anymore so she could see the bigger picture of how she could still serve, and serve well. The changes have been small and most likely invisible to my untrained eye, but they are there. The tree is not flashy in its groundedness, but I have found there is rarely anything sexy or attractive about building a life of resilience, especially while it's in the process of being cultivated for the purpose of turning horrible circumstances into meaningful contributions to the world.

It took me way too long to stop missing Africa in such a visceral way—but as I've learned, grief is not linear, and over time, the weight of grief, while it doesn't change in its heaviness, our ability to carry such heavy things does as we get stronger, as well as our ability to adapt to the new world around us. I can finally say, though, that I have learned to live with my grief over having lost the life I had worked so hard to cultivate, that I had spent so many years creating. It wasn't easy, and it wasn't fast, but it was—and is—possible.

Grief Can Be Your Path to Purpose

Grief is often seen as something that only takes from us—our sense of normalcy, our sense of safety, sometimes even our sense of self. But beneath the pain, grief also offers something unexpected: the opportunity to rebuild, to redefine, and to rediscover purpose in our lives.

When we experience loss, the world as we knew it shifts. What once felt certain no longer is, and the things that seemed important before may now feel trivial. In this disorienting space, we have a choice: to remain lost in the pain or to search for meaning within it. Grief forces us to ask: *What truly matters? What do I want my life to stand for? How can I honor what I have lost by how I choose to continue to live?*

With time, we begin to understand that resilience is not just about surviving—it is about using our survival as a foundation for something meaningful. Many of the most impactful people in history, the ones who have changed lives, created movements, and inspired transformation, were shaped by grief. They allowed their losses to guide them toward something greater than themselves.

There is a hidden power of grief: It strips us down to what is essential, and in that raw, vulnerable state, it gives us the clarity to build a life of deeper intention. It teaches us that our pain can have a purpose—not because suffering is necessary for growth, but because loss reminds us of what is truly valuable. Change is usually closely linked to loss and these two things are the most human reminders that we are still alive.

In the end, grief does not only make us more resilient; it makes us more purposeful. It pushes us to love more fiercely, to pursue what matters without hesitation, and to create something meaningful in the time we have. If we let it, grief can be the force that not only shapes us but also propels us forward into the most purposeful chapter of our lives.

Grief, above all, is not a punishment, but rather, our teacher.

Survivor Spotlight: Jennifer Collins—Surviving Survival When Others Don't

I met Jennifer several years ago at a fundraising event where I'd been invited to speak. It was one of those evenings where the room felt as big as the moment, and I remember feeling anxious, not quite sure what I was walking into. Then I was introduced to her. She was warm, grounded, and immediately put me at ease. We sat next to each other at dinner, and while I can't recall the names of most of the guests that night, I do remember how cold we were—our feet practically frozen to the floor beneath us. The dinner had been arranged on top of the frozen floor of a hockey stadium for the Dallas Stars. We laughed about how cold we were, shivering in our dresses and nibbling on salads. In that small moment of shared discomfort, a connection was formed.

Over the years, our paths continued to cross at events and gatherings. I had a general sense of her story, and how it connected to the cause we were both supporting, but it wasn't until I saw her take the stage and speak her truth out loud that I truly understood.

She told the story of her husband, a Navy SEAL—his service, his strength, and how something began to shift in him long after the visible battles had ended. What she described was something I've seen before, in other families, and even in my own: the slow unraveling that no one sees coming until it's already begun. The subtle changes and the growing distance, all suggesting that something is deeply wrong, but no one can name it or figure out what is causing it.

He was a high performer, like so many who serve—reliable, brave, the one everyone could count on. But over time, cracks began to appear. He became more anxious, more rigid. Sleep escaped him. Small tasks felt insurmountable. At first, it looked like stress, or burnout, or maybe the weight of too many deployments—but it was something else, Jennifer knew—there was something deeper. And when his career ended, the scaffolding that held him up seemed to collapse.

Jennifer did everything she could to help him—scheduled doctors' appointments, took him to scans, dragged him to clinics, all giving him diagnoses that didn't quite fit. It was like chasing a ghost in the dark. And then, one day, it was over. There was a message—a final goodbye. The last act from a man whose mind had become unfamiliar even to himself.

In her grief, Jennifer did something extraordinary; she looked for answers. She offered his story to science, to research, to the hope that maybe what they couldn't see on an MRI would reveal itself another way, and it did.

What was found in her husband's brain wasn't visible to the naked eye, or even to standard medical equipment. It was microscopic—scar tissue buried deep within the brain, caused by repeated exposure to low-level blasts. Not the dramatic kind from war movies, but the quieter, constant ones from training, from breaching, from the everyday work of Special Operations.

That discovery changed things. It gave shape to the invisible and it named the unnamable. Jennifer took that knowledge and turned it outward—reaching out to other families, sharing what she'd learned, helping others donate brains, find closure, and advocate for change.

I met with Jennifer virtually a few months ago, to talk to her about this book and explain why I felt so moved by her work both in the aftermath of her great loss, as well as for the Navy SEAL Legacy Foundation, for which she works. I figured we would talk about her mission to get more information to the military decision makers about the critical level of understanding of what combat does to our soldiers' brains, but our conversation took a different turn.

Jennifer, while not adhering to any type of religious dogma today, credits her ability to survive the tragic loss of her husband, and then continue on to find a space of purpose and thriving in the years that would follow, to the strong underpinnings of faith and family that she grew up with. The product of a large Irish Catholic family, she was raised in Philadelphia, and Jennifer counts herself incredibly blessed to have grown up with grandparents present in her everyday life, as well as having been surrounded by siblings, aunts and uncles, cousins—many who lived around the corner. Because she is from such a large family, it was inevitable that while she was surrounded by love, laughter, and beautiful memories, she also witnessed tremendous heartache at times throughout her most formative years. What she experienced in those difficult moments was a family coming together to create a sense of support and community, and she couldn't have known it then, but that would become the foundation for which Jennifer would need to survive survival as she worked to rebuild her own life in adulthood after the loss of her husband.

It was because of that sense of community that Jennifer was able to grieve, and then identify that she felt she had a responsibility to give back in the way that she did, not only to understand the impacts of combat on her own life, but for the military community, and in particular, the wives who were left behind with broken hearts and difficult questions that no one seemed to be able to answer.

While Jennifer has become the face of advocating for research and better awareness around traumatic brain injury and mental health for the military community, she revealed during our conversation that the route to turning her life's hardest moments into meaningful contribution for the world has been a messy, turbulent endeavor that has often left her wondering if she was doing the right thing. While her advocacy has brought understanding about the loss of these veterans and the pain they have endured into the necessary spotlight, she was very transparent about the often-less-talked-about effect of the intent versus impact for the survivors—the families of those who have been lost to suicide. I completely understood her take on the fact that nothing, not even in this scenario, is black and white. Things get really grey, especially where loss and grief are concerned.

Not one part of this journey has been easy for Jennifer or her children. But she has figured out a way to survive the survival through her work with the SEAL Legacy Foundation. She continues to share her and Dave's story to shine a light on the effects of combat and military life for those who remain living, and the way she does it is so strong and resolute while remaining compelling. When I think of someone who has survived the crushing experience of loss and grief and turned it into purpose, Jennifer's face is right next to the definition in that book. I'm inspired by her and the work she continues to do, and I am humbled by what she has had to give up in service to her country. While Dave will always be a hero, she, too, is an extraordinary one.

How Jennifer's Story Reflects the RISE Framework

Jennifer's story is a living testament to the strength it takes to hold grief and *still choose to build*. Through personal devastation, she has become a powerful advocate—not just for her husband's memory, but for the lives and futures of others navigating invisible wounds.

R - Reckon with the Pain

Jennifer didn't get to prepare for the kind of loss that found her. Her husband, a highly-trained Navy SEAL, deteriorated slowly and silently under the weight of invisible trauma. When he died by suicide, it shattered her world in a way no ceremony or script could contain, but she didn't hide from the heartbreak. She sat in it, questioned it, and wept through it.

Jennifer never pretended it was clean. Grief, for her, was messy, aching, complicated—and honest.

I - Identify the Impact

Jennifer didn't just lose her husband; she lost certainty, direction, and the scaffolding of a life she had built with him. In the absence of answers, she began searching: *What happened? Why? What now?* This search became a way of naming what grief had taken—and what it had left behind. She allowed herself to feel the grey, the guilt, the uncertainty. And slowly, she began to find her footing again.

S - Seek the Meaning

Meaning didn't come all at once, but it began to emerge through her advocacy. When Jennifer learned that her husband's symptoms were tied to blast-related brain trauma, she took that discovery and turned it into a mission, not just to honor Dave—but to protect and inform other military families. She turned her grief into a lighthouse.

E – Embody the Purpose

Jennifer is building something bigger than herself. Through her work with the SEAL Legacy Foundation, through supporting other widows, through showing up in spaces where silence used to reign—she is living a legacy that both honors and outlives the man she lost.

Her story reminds us: grief doesn't have to be hidden to be sacred; it can be shared. It can be moved through. It can even be offered. Jennifer shows us that surviving survival is not about forgetting what was lost—it's about *refusing to let that loss be the end of the story*.

PAUSE, PONDER, AND PROCESS

1. **What have you lost that still needs to be named?**
   Note that grief isn't always about a person—it can be the loss of who you were, what you hoped for, or the life you thought you'd have.

2. **How were you taught to express—or suppress—your grief?**
   Are you carrying beliefs that say you need to "be strong," "move on," or "keep it together"?

3. **What does your grief need from you right now?**
   Does it need rest, words, stillness, movement, or someone to witness it with you?

4. **Where have you felt unseen or misunderstood in your grief?**
   And who, if anyone, has helped you feel seen?

5. **What would it look like to stop trying to fix your grief, and instead tend to it?**
   How might your relationship with it shift?

6. **Can you name one small thing your grief has taught you about love, life, or yourself?**
   Not to minimize the pain—but to honor what grief might be revealing.

RISE Reminders:

- I don't have to rush my way through this—grief takes the time it needs.
- My sorrow is not a weakness; it's a reflection of how deeply I've loved.
- It's okay to be changed by this—grief rewrites us, and that's part of healing.
- Even in my pain, there is still something meaningful to hold onto.
- This grief is evidence that something mattered.

PART II
IDENTIFY THE IMPACT

CHAPTER 4
HINDSIGHT GIVES AND TAKES AWAY

*This isn't the final chapter. It's just a page
in the bigger story of your life—and you get to
decide what comes next.*
—Jessica C. Buchanan

"Why did this have to change everything, Dad?" I wept into the phone one afternoon while my youngest was napping and my toddler stared, transfixed by the animated dogs in superhero costumes on the television.

I was still deep in my grief and exhausted from the demands of my life in its current state. I had made a few mom friends by now, and we had settled into a nice rental in the historic district of Alexandria, Virginia. Erik was traveling for a consultancy gig he had secured and was en route to Africa for the next ten days.

People were astounded at the fact that I was okay with him picking up and going back to "the scene of the crime," especially when it wasn't just about us anymore; we had two kids to care for and protect. I had a hard time understanding why I was okay with it myself, and therefore, could not explain to inquirers that actually, I wasn't okay with him going back, but not for the reasons they expected. Rather than being driven by fear that something terrible was going to happen to him while he was continuing his international development work, I was consumed by insane amounts of jealousy over him getting to keep his job, and, thus, his identity and purpose. It was utterly paralyzing and seeped into every part of our relationship.

Here he was, riding off into the African sunset, doing what he had always done, continuing to be the Somalia expert, living his best life, and earning an income for our family while going to all our favorite restaurants in Nairobi, meeting our friends for coffees as he traveled his way through my beloved city, while I was left behind in DC, in charge of changing poopy diapers, wiping snotty noses, and unable to find time to shower on most days. I went from doing work that was visible and mattered to actual people and governments to spending my days doing important work, yes, but largely invisible and ignored by the outside world.

When I was at my lowest points, I would guilt myself into gratitude. *Jess*, I would admonish. *You have been given your life back by SEAL Team Six—think of all the people that put their lives on the line for you! You should be more grateful!* But the truth was, and it was hard for me to admit this, even to my therapist, that it was a life I no longer recognized and a life I had not asked for. On the worst days, I wasn't sure if it was the life I wanted.

While I was sitting out there for all those days in the desert as a hostage, I knew it was taking a toll on my mental health, for sure, but I had no idea the experience was going to change everything about my life in the aftermath. I thought, very naively, that I would reunite with my husband and my family, take a vacation, go to therapy a couple of times, and then drop back into my life as it was—minus the fieldwork in Somalia. Boy, was I wrong.

Part of this, of course, had to do with the reality that I got pregnant a few days after the rescue and was completely thrown into motherhood without getting a chance to catch my breath, rest, and heal. Becoming a parent, in the best of circumstances, is world altering—and in my situation, it flipped everything about my life upside down and left the pieces scattered.

I was no longer a working professional based in East Africa, fully employed to use my expertise in education to write a curriculum on mine risk education for ministries of education of newly organized countries. I was no longer hopping on UN planes to go and train staff on the dangers of landmines and helping them communicate those lessons to nonliterate people groups in the countries we worked in. I was no longer meeting friends I adored for brunch on Saturday mornings at my favorite restaurants in Nairobi, or getting to go to my yoga class led by a Hindi spiritual teacher at a Hindu temple. And at its most primitive, I could no longer sleep through the night or walk down the street without being in fight or flight mode and always looking over my shoulder.

I had decided at some point in the aftermath of the kidnapping that I wasn't going to waste time trying to answer the unanswerable question: *Why did this happen to me?* In a way, I knew why it had happened. I hadn't listened to my intuition. I had deferred my personal safety to my organization, and they had been remiss in their duty of care and withheld critical information from me about an active kidnapping threat on the organization. I knew something was off and had tried to cancel the training, but unable to determine the difference between intuition and paranoia, I gave in, and it changed my life.

So, as a result, I didn't spend a whole lot of time pondering the more esoteric "Why did this have to happen to me?" question, but rather, I concentrated on another form, which led me, ironically, to the same dead end.

"Why did it have to *change* everything?" I whined to my Dad again as I hit play on the television remote so my toddler could watch the next episode. I rattled off the list of things that had changed in my life because of the kidnapping: my job, my purpose, my home, my role in that home. My summary was met with a few moments of silence, which wasn't unusual for my dad. He's a thinker and careful with his words; he is one of those rarities who really does "think before he talks." I knew he had something important to say when he cleared his throat from the other end of the line.

"You know, Jess, you're not the only one in the world who has had your life upended by change you didn't choose. All the things you are describing are things I have experienced after we lost your mother. Many people experience events in their lives that change everything. What they choose to do in the aftermath differentiates the victims from the victors—whether you are going just to keep surviving or move into thriving."

Tears streamed down my face as I tried to recover from the feeling that the wind had been knocked out of me. His truth hurt. I was interrupted from my pity party when my two-year-old approached me, demanding a snack. As I moved to the kitchen searching for

Goldfish crackers, I made an excuse to get off the phone and quickly hung up before sobs overtook me.

I got Auggie settled in with his crackers, and then forced myself to sit with the conversation. In his loving way, my dad was telling me I needed to get over myself and realize I wasn't that special. Everyone is surviving something, is what he was saying. Or they have, or they will. This is the human experience, and no one is exempt. The all-important question I hadn't had space in my heart to ponder, because I had been consumed with the relentless wondering of *why* had this changed everything, was what would I do with what was left of it?

* * *

I wish I could say I quickly made a change, and the next week, I was walking around with my head held high, deciding to stop feeling sorry for myself. Now, before you get defensive on my behalf for being so hard on myself, you have to understand that years had passed by this point, and I can see in hindsight, because who doesn't love that 20/20 vision, that I was indeed very comfortable floating around in the pool of "unrealized possibilities." Much to my husband's frustration, I had an unusually well-developed skill of remembering things as I wanted to remember them instead of acknowledging how things really were. I spent years waxing and waning about the "good old days" as I sobbed alone in the bathtub at night after I had put my kids to bed. I had been given so much, and yet, I felt I had been robbed—and violently so. Don't get me wrong—there were things I liked about the life I was building—my kids, relative safety, and Target—I was a pro at remembering how things used to be and using it as permission to splash around in victimhood. No one faulted me for this. My God, no one demanded that I get up off my keister and start a foundation or cure cancer or make my life "worth" the saving by SEAL Team Six. I think people would have understood if I wanted to reside in my bed and live out my days from under my duvet.

But when I got frank with myself, I knew that wasn't what I wanted. I wanted to find a way to go back to my old life, to be the Africa Jess that I had been before the kidnapping had taken over seemingly every facet of my being. But how?

* * *

I pulled to a slow stop at the red light and couldn't help but notice the way the autumn sun cast warm glowing rays of light that stretched across my dashboard. I closed my eyes and just allowed myself a brief second to feel the warmth of the sun on my skin. Life was moving so quickly, and I often pined for long, quiet stretches of solitude, which were impossible to find in my current phase of life.

I had been teaching at the local elementary school for about a year, and while it was fun, I could feel my excitement fading with each morning I schlepped through the school doors. When my son started kindergarten the year before, I decided it was time to return to work full-time. Since I hadn't figured out what else I could do besides teaching, I applied for the position as outdoor education coordinator at his school, even though I wasn't sure that was what I wanted to do or if I knew that much about growing things. The kids were cute, but it was backbreaking work; being outside no matter the weather conditions, with kids of all ages from various countries, at all hours of the morning and afternoon, was taxing. Trying to keep them from hurting themselves and from making a break for it when not contained within the four walls of their classroom was no small task. I firmly believed in nature's benefits to foster meaningful educational experiences for kids, and as far as teaching goes, it felt like the right fit, until it didn't.

I had carefully weighed the pros and cons of returning to the education field once my baby started sleeping through the night. The pros included the benefits of being on the same schedule as my children, which is why my mother encouraged me so often to pursue a degree in teaching in the first place. So, I dutifully pursued the career of a public school teacher, following my mother's advice.

Since my schedule matched my children's exactly, I had zero minutes to myself on any given day and even less time to address the domestic needs of family life. This solo trip to the grocery store was a rarity, and I was drinking up the alone time. Somewhere in the space between my mind wandering off and the car behind me lying on its horn, signaling to me that it was time to move, a truth was illuminated to me. In that moment, as I was turning left off of Fort Hunt Road, heading home on that warm September afternoon, I realized I could never be truly fulfilled doing the job I had been doing before the kidnapping. It had never occurred to me that I could not fit into a job designed for the pre-trauma version of myself. I had been stretched and reshaped into another person, beyond previous recognition, at least on the inside, and the stuff of life from "before" would never do. Not only did the work I used to do teaching mine risk education and community safety to nonliterate people groups in East Africa not fit in my current environment, it was clear I had been changed on a cellular level, and just like my postpartum body was not ever going to fit back into those skinny jeans I loved so much, I realized I would never fit back into that old life that I had worked so hard to cultivate. As much as I loved the work I used to do, the people I served, the traveling across the world—that was then, and this was now.

My purpose would have to change to fit the trauma-sized hole in my heart.

* * *

It would be some time before I could answer the question: *Why did this thing have to change everything?* I know now, but I don't want to spoil the book for you! What I do want to say at this point, however, is that if you, too, have been through a life-changing disaster, a traumatic or extraordinary experience that has changed you on a cellular level, and you are stuck in the rumination of "Why did this have to happen to *me*?" I humbly come to you with the offer of a reframe. Instead of continuing down the path that will get you nowhere, I invite you to stop asking, "Why did this happen to *me*?" and try asking instead, "Why *not* me?"

Here's what I know about life: it's no respecter of persons. *No one* gets through it without experiencing a hardship. Part of the human experience is about forming resilience and learning who we are and what we are all about in the face of extraordinary challenges—if we make it. It doesn't seem fair, but it's the reality, and I am of the mindset that what doesn't kill us makes us stronger, and isn't that the whole point? To grow strong? We go to the gym to build strength, we work our Sodoku puzzles to build memory muscle, we go to university to create intellectual endurance . . . and so on. Why would life not give us the opportunity to build our emotional and spiritual tenacity in this way?

So I ask you again: *Why not you?* You cannot run, and you cannot hide, no matter how much money, education, community, or intelligence you possess. What matters at the end of the day is what we choose to do with it all once it has happened, or sometimes in real-time while it is all unfolding in all its gritty glory.

When I got off that phone call with my dad so many years ago, I found a quiet spot and probably turned on another episode of something to entertain my toddler—it may not have been my finest moment as a mother, but he's twelve now, and he seems fine! I thought about everything my dad had been through in the last couple of years since the sudden loss of my mother, his wife of over thirty-two years. He had lost his life partner, his friend, his lover, and the mother of his children. Subsequently, he lost his home and his direction as to where he should be, as my mother died six months after they moved to their retirement spot. He had left his social life and church community to build a new one with my mother, and as an extreme introvert who relied on my mother's people skills to build a social network, he was at a complete loss.

Yes, his life had been upended too, and he had been changed by tragedy—because not only had my mom passed suddenly, but just a little over a year later, I had been kidnapped, and he thought he was going to lose me too. As I cataloged all the ways in which his life had changed so fundamentally, I could see the parallels that I hadn't noticed before because, quite frankly, I had been so consumed with my pain that I couldn't be bothered with anyone else's. It was the perspective shift I needed, and I will continue returning to that baseline when I struggle to understand why something that has happened in my life isn't what I would have chosen.

When I spent more time with this question, I could take the kidnapping and the following ramifications less personally. I think one of the things that keeps people stuck in victim mode is the subconscious belief that it is personal—as if God, the Universe, or some cosmic meany has picked them up and thrown them across the football field of life, just for the fun of it.

I believe that we are not alone here; we have divine providence that is loving and provides for us—and I know that doesn't work for everyone. However, I believe that the bad things that happen to us are meant to be learning opportunities that build our character, develop our inner strength, and lead us down the path of our true purpose. If we spend all our time and energy pounding our fists on the ground and throwing our spite into the air at wanting answers to the questions of "Why did this horrible thing happen to me?" then we are missing the point, as well as the opportunity.

Here's a secret I learned long ago: we're not special. I mean, we are unique, worthy, and divine, but none of us is unique enough to be picked on by a big cosmic genie. One of my favorite quotes by the wise and so-incredibly-talented-that-her-quote-makes-me-weep author Brianna Wiest is, "Sometimes, you get what you want. Other times you get a lesson in patience, timing, alignment, empathy, compassion, faith, perseverance, resilience, humility, trust, meaning, awareness, resistance, purpose, clarity, grief, beauty, and life. Either way, you win."

If you are ready to consider what is beyond surviving, I'd challenge you to start there. Try asking yourself, "Why *not* me?" instead of "Why *me?*" and see what happens next.

* * *

There's a difference between acceptance and surrender. You can't have one without the other, because surrender can't happen until acceptance occurs.

We often use these words interchangeably so I think it's essential to understand the difference and what it looks like in our lives when we are trying to move through our toughest moments.

Acceptance means we are acknowledging the reality of our situation without resistance. It is what it is, whether they are reasonable, bad, or neutral. Acceptance happens when we stop fighting with whatever is taking place and release ourselves from thinking about how we will solve the problem every second of every day. It doesn't mean we've given up, and I believe that deep down inside, many people are afraid to accept a diagnosis, prognosis, divorce papers, or (you can fill in the blank) because they are worried that if they stop fighting, emotionally and physically, that they will have given up. It's quite the opposite because once you accept what has happened, this new reality you didn't choose, you can then select as to how you want to move forward—how you are going to respond. You can adjust, adapt, or act, which will look different for everyone.

Surrender is our "Jesus take the wheel moment." It's that moment when we are at the end of our rope, exhausted from railing against this new reality, and we throw our hands up in the air and relinquish control. We decide to trust the process and walk by faith and decide we don't have the strength to control the outcome anymore, and we will have to wait it out.

One of the most potent moments of surrender I have ever witnessed was the morning after my mother passed away. We had lost her suddenly, tragically, six days after her fifty-seventh birthday, and we were in the most significant state of shock we had ever experienced as a family. My father, a person of deep faith and great spirituality, asked my siblings and me to gather in the kitchen, around the table, where we spent so much time together growing up. My mother was from southern Indiana, and her fried chicken was renowned. It seemed only natural to gather in the place where she spent so much time caring for us. I will never forget my father asking us to pray with him and the way he gripped the top rungs of the kitchen chair, knuckles whitening as if that chair was the only thing holding him upright. Not one to give public displays of emotion, I silently wept as I watched my father struggle to take a breath and get his prayer out. After an uncontrollable sob, he simply prayed, "God, I don't understand you. But I choose to trust you."

That prayer carried my family through some very dark days, and while I didn't know it then, those words would become my mantra as I languished in the desert during my ninety-three-day captivity. I would walk in circles around my mat, whispering to the sky in panic, "God, I don't understand, but I choose to trust. God, I don't understand why this is happening, but I choose to trust you."

Every time I said that prayer to myself, even in some of the most terrifying moments, I would focus on the peace that surpassed all understanding that would come over me. Did it make me want to stay in the desert surrounded by thirty crazed pirates? Heck no. Did allowing that peace that came from my act of surrender tempt me into just giving up? Absolutely not. If anything, it made me feel stronger and more resolved to survive this ordeal so I could continue to live and understand my purpose.

Trusting is not giving up, sweet friend. It's letting go of control you don't have anyway and letting life lead you through the darkness so you can one day shine your light on life.

Steps to Restoration: Acknowledge and Surrender

Maybe prayer doesn't work for you. Perhaps you don't believe in a higher power or any of that stuff and you are wondering how you can surrender your pain to something you don't believe in. Or maybe you once believed in a God or higher power, and circumstances that have brought so much pain and transition into your life have left you doubting. Wherever you are at, I do believe you can trust that life is not out to get you, and that there is a purpose for all your pain. But you won't get there if you refuse to accept the reality of what is and if you cannot figure out a way to surrender your heartache to life.

Everyone has to find their own way, and I would argue that *that* is exactly the point.

Below, I have listed seven steps I took to get to a place of surrender in my healing journey. Again, I am offering these up simply so that you can have an idea of what worked for me. Please read through the following questions and decide what resonates. For the points that do not, I encourage you to do some reflection and journaling as to why they do not. This is a judgment-free zone. All I am asking you to do is consider and reflect.

I had to recognize what I was resisting. After I was rescued, the outside world thought the hard part was over. But I experienced something so much different. What I resisted most wasn't the trauma of the ninety-three days—I had already survived that. It was the truth that my life, my identity, my sense of safety would never go back to what they were before. I wanted to bounce back, to pretend I was okay. I didn't want to admit how broken I felt inside. I had to sit with things and really ponder. It took courage to ask myself questions like: What truth am I struggling to face about what I've lived through? Where am I pretending I'm fine when I'm actually hurting? What am I afraid will happen if I stop resisting?

I had to allow myself to feel. During captivity, I had no choice but to numb myself to survive. But once I was home, the emotions I had buried came flooding in—fear, rage, sadness, guilt. For a long time, I tried to outrun them, but healing didn't begin until I gave myself permission to *feel it all*. I had to cry. I had to rage. I had to collapse. And slowly, feeling made room for something else: release.

It was scary to ponder the feelings that I was so afraid of, because frankly, I was scared I would lose my mind to what I hadn't faced. But I decided to take the feelings in little increments and over time, my ability to withstand the discomfort grew. It was life changing for me to learn that emotional pain actually subsides after ninety seconds. According to Dr. Jill Bolte Taylor, a Harvard-trained neuroanatomist, when we experience an intense emotion, our brain triggers a biochemical response that surges through the body. If we don't add new thoughts to re-trigger the emotion, that physical wave (the racing heart, the tight chest, the heat in our face) will naturally subside in just a minute and a half. It's not about avoiding our emotions, but allowing them to rise, crest, and pass like a wave. When I practiced observing my feelings, even just for ninety seconds, I began to reclaim control when I experienced what has become one of my most fundamental truths: nothing lasts forever, not even those moments of anxiety and panic that are associated with the painful memories that inevitably occur on our healing journeys.

It's Possible to Shift from "Why Me?" to "Now What?"

I asked, "Why me?" a thousand times. Why was I taken? Why was I spared? Why did I live when others didn't? But those questions never gave me peace. The turning point came when I began asking different questions: Now what? What do I do with this pain? Who can I help by telling the truth of what I've endured? That shift changed everything. It gave my pain a place to go. Believe me, I was stuck in the "Why me? Why did it have to change everything?" space for a long time. But when I got through to the other side and was able to ask myself, "Now what?" it felt hopeful; there was a small promise tucked away inside me that took on the meaning I needed in order to see light where there had been so much darkness.

I decided to stop fighting reality. I wanted my life back. I wanted the nightmares to stop. I wanted the story to be over. But the moment I stopped fighting what had happened—stopped trying to erase it—and instead *integrated it*, I began to soften. Captivity became a chapter, not my whole book. It was part of my becoming, not the definition of my identity. It was a difficult question to answer when I sat with it: *What reality am I still trying to rewrite or escape?* And the answers were complicated. But the next question I asked myself helped me discover what true acceptance in our lives can feel like—I wasn't in agreement with what had happened. I wasn't saying it was okay, or that my life was better off for it—no way! But I did have the strength to recognize that I was brave enough to let this be an incredibly important part of my story without letting it be the end.

I had to reframe the situation because the word "victim" never sat right with me. I wanted to be more than what had happened to me. When I reframed my experience as a calling—to speak, to write, to walk beside others in their pain—I began to feel powerful again. My captivity gave me clarity about what mattered to me. It stripped away the unimportant. I wouldn't have chosen it—but I could choose what I did with it. I get a lot of backlash when I write about this concept on social media; I understand when people are in the throes of their pain that this is an impossible concept to embrace, but I started considering the idea that perhaps all of this "stuff" had happened *for* me, and not *to* me. Was there a small part of me that could believe that I hadn't been kidnapped as a punishment, but rather as a means of preparation for a call on my life that was bigger than I could imagine? I sit here today, writing these words, because I am the direct recipient of the truth: anything is possible. *Anything.*

I finally had to take action. But it didn't start with a big, bold move. It began quietly, almost invisibly—with what thought leader Glennon Doyle calls "the next right thing." For me, that meant pulling the covers off in the morning when I'd rather stay hidden. It meant writing a single sentence, even if it wasn't perfect. Making one phone call, even if my voice trembled. Those small steps felt like nothing at the time, but they were everything. They were movement. And eventually, they became bigger things: launching a podcast, standing on stages, writing a book. I never felt fully ready—I just showed up and did the next right thing anyway.

Along the way, I started asking myself different questions—not the kind that demanded a five-year plan, but the kind that invited presence and compassion. *What's one small, concrete action I can take today toward healing or purpose?* Sometimes the answer was "breathe" or "drink water" or "text a friend." *What would it look like to take one brave step, even if I still feel broken?* It looked like speaking up when it would've been easier to stay quiet. Like telling my story before I felt polished or healed. And maybe the most powerful question of all: *What have I already done that I haven't given myself credit for?* Because survival itself is no small thing.

Neither is choosing to try again. Each time I paused to ask these questions, I saw myself more clearly—not as someone waiting to become whole, but as someone already walking the path. And that's when I finally let myself ask: *Now what?* Now that I know I can survive, now that I've seen my own strength—what will I do with it?

Self-compassion is essential to surviving survival. I remember one morning, years after I was rescued, finding myself on the floor of my closet, surrendering to a massive panic attack. My husband and I were arguing about something, nothing too serious, just regular, run-of-the-mill life stuff when I found myself paralyzed by a wave of fear I couldn't explain. Nothing had really happened—I couldn't find an exact trigger I could name. But my body remembered and demanded attention. My first instinct was frustration at myself—*You should be over this by now!* I chastised myself as I wiped tears with the cuff of a pant leg hanging down. But then, something softer rose up within me: *What if this isn't about fixing yourself, Jess? What if it's about befriending yourself?* I pictured what I would say to a friend in that same moment—phrases like, *You're safe now. You've come so far. It's okay to rest*, came to my mind. So I did. Once I calmed down, I climbed out of the closet, apologized to my husband and went to the kitchen to make a cup of tea. I wrapped myself in a blanket, settled in on the couch with my three-year-old and canceled everything we had planned for that day. I didn't do this because I was weak, but because I was learning to be kind to the version of me that had survived. That, too, is healing, and I think we often overlook that significant progress. And when the shame crept in, I asked: *Why do I need permission to rest, to grieve, or even to feel proud?* Sometimes, the bravest thing we can do is meet ourselves with gentleness—especially on the days we feel we haven't earned it.

PAUSE, PONDER, AND PROCESS ACCEPTANCE

1. **How does the following statement resonate with you?**
   Acceptance is about acknowledging reality without resistance and making peace with what is.

2. **What *is* your current reality right now? What *is*?**
   Be honest as you can be . . .

3. **Do you think there is a universe where you could ever be at peace with what is? Why or why not?**

4. **What do you think you would need to get to a place of peace within your current reality?**

5. **Ask yourself: *What am I struggling to accept?* Is it a situation, emotion, past event, or something beyond your control that is causing you to hold on so tightly?**
   Write about it!

6. **According to renowned researcher and doctor Gabor Maté, the most suppressed emotions are rage, anger, and grief. Suppressing emotions makes acceptance harder, and it weakens our immune system. In order to get to the point of acceptance, you have to give yourself permission to grieve, feel frustration, or process pain and disappointment—things take the time they need to take. Instead of asking, *"Why did this happen?"* I'd love for you to try to shift to, *"Okay, this has happened. Is it possible to move forward? Do I even want to move forward?***

If you decide you want to move forward, and that there is a slight chance it could be possible, then how are you going to do it? Reframing this question can keep you from getting stuck in a pattern of rumination which is not going to do anyone any favors.

7. **What are you ruminating over right now? How is it helping you? How is it keeping you from finding peace?**

8. **Is resisting in the acceptance of _____ making you suffer more?**
   Here's the thing: This is happening, whether you like it or not. You can fight it, or you can move with it.

9. **Is there any part of this situation where you can find autonomy in this life-changing event?**
   According to research conducted by BetterUp, we are *six* times more likely to cultivate strong resilience in the middle of a life changing event if we can create our own choice and autonomy in the middle of it. If it is beyond your control, here is your chance to practice letting go of the outcome.

10. **Acceptance is excruciatingly hard. Self-compassion is key. What loving words can you write for yourself here about how you are doing at accepting this situation that you did not choose?**
    Surrender is about acknowledging the pain, grief or hardship without being consumed by the struggle against it. This does not mean you are a passive bystander or victim to your pain, but rather, you choose to respond with awareness, trust and resilience rather than fear or resistance.

PAUSE, PONDER, AND PROCESS SURRENDER

1. **Can you let go of the need to control?**
   I know . . . it's easier said than done! What is yours to manage and what isn't? Are you grieving over the loss of a relationship or a curveball thrown at your career? What is within *your* control, and what is *not*?

2. **Trust that life is unfolding as it should.**
   Surrender doesn't mean giving up—it means trusting that things will work out, even if you can't see how yet, and most importantly, that you stop giving energy to trying to change things that you cannot. One of my favorite questions ever is, *What if this is happening for me, not to me?* People get really triggered by this question . . . but I feel it has helped me so much as I've tried to reframe the hard things.

   What if this is happening *for* you, and not *to* you? Does that make you want to throw this book across the room? Or does it bring you some comfort?

3. **Practice presence.**
   Stop obsessing over what could have been and start embracing where you are right now. Again, easier said than done, I know.

   How can you anchor yourself in the present moment? Can you focus on your breath? Can you stop what you are doing and take in your surroundings? What can you do right now to bring yourself into the present?

4. Develop a surrender mantra.
I've already shared a couple of mine with you, such as:
- Things take the time they need to take. No more, no less.
- I don't understand. But I choose to trust.
- Things don't happen to me. Things happen for me.

Here are a few others I find immensely helpful.
- I trust the process of life.
- I surrender to the flow of what is.
- I release my need to control everything.

Can you try to write your own? I would encourage you to write this down and put it where you are going to see it all the time. One thing I do is personalize my morning alarm with a mantra so that the first thing I see in the morning when I turn the alarm off is this reminder.

5. Practice big surrender by surrendering in small ways daily.
- Let go of minor irritations (e.g., traffic, delays, annoying people).
- Release attachment to people's opinions.
- Trust that things don't have to go exactly as planned for them to turn out okay.

Can you start taking a few moments at the end of the day to reflect on all the ways you have surrendered your need for control to life? I am guessing that chronicling all the small ways might bolster your faith in yourself to surrender some of the bigger things.

> **6. Align with something bigger than yourself.**
> Whether through faith, nature, or the universe, I believe it is critically important that we find something bigger than ourselves to trust in. Who or what do you believe in? Does that bring you peace?

Survivor Spotlight: Gabriela Q. Bell—The View Is Still the View

What if it didn't happen *to* you, but *for* you?

It's a question that can feel cruel when you're lying on the floor—figuratively or literally—crushed beneath the weight of betrayal, heartbreak, or survival. But it's a question that, over time, many survivors come to ask. Not to minimize the pain, but to search for the possibility inside it. To ask, "Is there something sacred I can carry forward from this wreckage?"

Gabriela Q. Bell's story is a stunning example of this shift.

For years, Gabi lived in a reality so common it's almost invisible: the unseen war zone of an abusive marriage. A military spouse, mother of four, and once an ambitious professional, she slowly became a shell of herself—cut off from income, from freedom, from basic human dignity. She stayed through pregnancies, postpartum depression, deployments, and unpredictable rages. Not because she lacked strength, but because she had so much of it—and used it all to protect her children, keep the peace, and hold her family together.

But the turning point came wrapped in devastation. When her husband cleared out their bank accounts and prepared to move the family overseas under his full financial control, Gabi made a split-second, life-defining decision: *I won't go.* She knew that if she boarded that plane, she would never be free. And so, with nothing but four children, six suitcases, two cats, a parrot, and a deep well of invisible courage, she began again.

It was messy, terrifying, and in the end, empowering.

In those early days, Gabi relied on friends and fellow military spouses. She picked furniture from the curb and fed her kids with what little she could scrape together. She taught part-time, took online courses, and got creative with side gigs. But something began to stir inside her—a whisper of the woman she had once been.

That whisper became a roar during her time at Dog Tag, Inc., a nonprofit program for veterans, military spouses, and caregivers. There, she didn't just learn business strategy—she reclaimed her voice. And with that voice, she built Organized Q, a remote staffing company designed to give other women in unpredictable life seasons the chance to earn a living on their terms.

It started with just Gabi—answering emails between hospital visits when her daughter had a medical emergency or when she had to wait in between sessions on court dates, working at kitchen tables and in school pick-up lines. But slowly, the business grew. One client became five. One assistant became a team. And now, Organized Q employs over twenty-five people, has doubled revenue year after year, and is projected to reach seven figures within two years.

This didn't happen *to* Gabi. In a strange, sacred way, it happened *for* her—and for every woman who has since found work, dignity, and possibility through the doors she kicked open.

And yet, even now, Gabi is clear: This isn't a hero story. It's a human one. She still hears echoes of past abuse in the quiet of the night. She still carries the weight of being the one holding it all together. But now she knows the truth: She is no longer trapped. She is building. She is leading. She is healing. And her children are thriving because she chose to survive her survival.

Sometimes, when we dare to ask, "What if this happened *for* me?" we discover a purpose we never would have chosen—but one that was waiting for us all along.

How Gabi's Story Reflects the RISE Framework
R - Reckon with the Pain

Gabi had to face the brutal truth of her reality: a home ruled by emotional, financial, and psychological abuse. For years, she stayed quiet—buffering her children from the rage, while silently erasing her own voice. Reckoning came slowly, in layers. But eventually, she saw her silence for what it was: survival, not weakness.

I - Identify the Impact

She began to name what had been lost—her financial independence, her self-trust, her health, and her identity beyond wife and mother. And she began to recognize the deeper toll: living in a constant state of fear had taught her to shrink, to disappear. But it had also taught her resilience, resourcefulness, and adaptability—the very traits she would later build her business on.

S - Seek the Meaning

When her plans were derailed again—this time by her daughter's medical crisis—Gabi didn't collapse. She listened to the whisper of purpose stirring in her. What if all this hardship was trying to show her the next step? What if the chaos had prepared her to create something for others who were struggling too? Out of necessity and vision, Organized Q was born.

E - Embody the Purpose

Today, Gabi embodies the kind of leader she once longed for—compassionate, clear-eyed, and bold. She employs other women facing invisible barriers, uses her platform to advocate for survivors, and models a new kind of success: one that makes space for tiredness, tenderness, and truth. Her life now reflects the meaning she chose to make from what tried to destroy her.

RISE Reminders:

- Every loss can carve space for something more honest to grow.
- I can become the safe place in which I am searching for.
- I carry wisdom now that only this path could have taught me.

PART III
SEEK THE MEANING

CHAPTER 5
THE ALCHEMY OF MEANING

In the first few pages of my *New York Times* bestseller *Impossible Odds*, the scene begins with a serious conversation between my husband and me, as we deliberate the threat level of going into Galkayo, Somalia. My company had me scheduled for the three-day training and neither of us felt good about it. After much deliberation, we finally decided, "What's the worst that could happen?" He'd worked in Somalia for years, and I had been there for nearly three. It wasn't the safest environment, but we were used to it and aware of most of the risks (you can't make a decision about personal safety when critical information is withheld from you, but I digress!).

The morning of October 25, 2011, I woke up around five a.m., with the call to prayer coming from the mosque next to the guesthouse. I was dripping with sweat because I had been having nightmares all night. Not a prolific dreamer, they were clear as real life with our compound being taken over by pirates rumored to be living in a house not too far away. There was a feeling behind the events in my dream that they had discovered that an American was staying on the premises, and they seized their opportunity—it was only hours before it actually happened.

In reality, I jumped at a loud bang on my door. My colleague was signaling it was time to get up and go to breakfast; just as I had been dreaming the pirates were banging on my door to take me away. Exhausted and hung over from staying up too late with Poul and drinking several glasses of white wine, I dragged my tired body to the bathroom and looked at myself in the mirror. I stared at my exhausted face and asked myself the question that will forever be one of the most important questions I have ever asked myself:

"Jess, do you want to do this?"

I was nervous about what was to come that day. We had already conducted two trainings, which had occurred on the compound where we stayed. Therefore, we were not required to be in transit. I knew from the Hostile Environmental Awareness Training I had participated in that I was most vulnerable when I was moving from one location to the other, and this third and final day of the training required us to leave the safety of the compound. Surprisingly, the Land Cruisers carrying our armed guards were on time, ready to take us over the Green Line. We drove to this neutral boundary that divided the town, two opposing clans governing their respective sides. As we stepped out of the vehicles to cross the boundary by foot, my senses were heightened and I kept looking around. I felt vulnerable and on the verge of panic. It took everything in me not to run to the other set of Land Cruisers that had been hired to take us the rest of the way to the south office for the training. We arrived without any incident, and I took my place at the head of the class as the regional education advisor and spent the day training our staff on the new community safety material I had developed for them to take out into the surrounding villages.

We stopped for lunch at noon, and I passed on the greasy plates of goat meat and rice, thinking I would eat something more appetizing at the guesthouse when we returned. Once the Land Cruisers finally arrived to take us back, we said our goodbyes to the staff and climbed in; I was ready to go. I breathed a long, slow sigh of relief as we pulled out of the compound's gates. We had made it through the entire day without anything happening! I was so relieved! All I could think about was what sort of workout I would do when I got back and what we would have for dinner—my stomach was rumbling loudly. As we meandered through the crowded streets of Galkayo, I texted my husband and checked on a few work emails. Suddenly, the driver slammed on the brakes and my head was propelled forward as another vehicle pulled up on our right side, cutting us off, splashing mud up all over our windows and windshield so we couldn't see. The driver looked confused as he sat up straight in his seat and began to roll his window down.

"What a jerk! Who drives like that?" I asked no one in particular. And then I could hear the voices of several Somali men—and they were angry. The voices were getting closer as if they were surrounding the vehicle, and then I felt the slam of the butt of an AK-47 on the car hood; it reverberated throughout the entire vehicle. Before I could process what was happening, the back door flung open; on the other side of that door was a furious man dressed in a police uniform, pointing his weapon right at my head. Without realizing it, I had been driven into a whole different life.

It would take me well into captivity before I would remember that conversation I had with myself the morning the kidnapping took place. It would take months of being terrorized by pirates and being driven around in the backcountry of the Somali desert before I remembered the moment I had so clearly abandoned myself. It would take me many years into my healing journey to understand that what had happened to me out there was the biggest lesson the Universe wanted to teach me. I'm not sure how I feel about lifetimes and such. Still, suppose there is one thing I am supposed to learn in this one. In that case, it is that repeated self-abandonment, entrenched in me by organized religion, my controlling mother, as well as just society at large, was going to be the death of me, literally. I had been taken out into the desert to learn the biggest lesson of my life: My intuition was always right, and I could trust it.

* * *

Life is either a lesson or a blessing; sometimes, it's both at the same time, and always it's both if we are open to receiving it. I don't think things happen just randomly and for no good reason. The hard things we face have been put in our path to teach us something; sometimes, the message is a little louder than others, but for me, the message was clear: This pattern was ready to be put to rest. The lesson I needed to learn about listening to my inner wisdom and reclaiming my voice has been empowering—it has forced me to face some hard truths about my repeated actions of deference and lack of personal responsibility. Mining the meaning from our life's most challenging moments is not about finding the silver lining or hanging out in the space of toxic positivity. I am not suggesting we dismiss all the pain and grief to focus on a "There's always a reason!" mindset (there *is* always purpose to be found, but that is not always a helpful narrative to follow in the beginning). Instead, I am inviting you into a practice whereby you can contemplate the underlying causes, perhaps even link them to other decisions you have made throughout your life, both bad and good, and evaluate what you want to do with these lessons moving forward.

* * *

Surviving a traumatic experience is no small feat. But survival alone is not the end of the journey—it is the beginning of a new path. Trauma leaves an imprint, but it also offers the raw material for transformation. The challenge is learning how to mine meaning from what you have endured and turn it into something that not only serves your healing but also contributes to the world.

Meaning-making does not happen passively; it is an active process. You must decide to engage with your experience, extract the lessons, and shape your story into a tool for growth. This chapter will guide you through that process, helping you reclaim your voice and use it as a force for good.

Scientific research supports the powerful role that meaning-making plays in healing from trauma. According to a 2020 review published in *Frontiers in Psychology*, individuals who engage in meaning-making after trauma experience greater psychological well-being, including reduced symptoms of PTSD and depression. The study found that meaning-making serves as a protective factor, enhancing resilience and fostering posttraumatic growth (PTG).

In fact, the concept of PTG—coined by psychologists Richard Tedeschi and Lawrence Calhoun—describes the positive psychological change that occurs as a result of the struggle with highly challenging life circumstances. Their research shows that people who reflect on their trauma and actively seek meaning from it are more likely to report increased personal strength, deeper relationships, and a stronger sense of life purpose.

A 2018 study published in the *Journal of Traumatic Stress* revealed that people who engage in narrative reframing—retelling their trauma story through a lens of strength and growth—experience a marked decrease in distress over time. This process helps individuals feel more in control of their story, fosters self-compassion, and reduces shame.

For so long, I had this compulsion to make my kidnapping experience mean something. I spent many years trying to figure out how to use it to uncover the next phase of my purpose. I spun my wheels and journaled in frustration—the harder I tried, the more confused I became. I didn't know then what I have since uncovered; to make something life-changing mean something for your life moving forward, you must first, figure out what it all means. Can you trace back through the experience you survived and connect the dots to the lessons you are meant to learn?

Remember all that talk about "Why did this happen to me?" and "Why not me?" stuff in chapter four? And then how I got so stuck on the gerbil wheel of why the kidnapping had to change everything? After many years of contemplation and soul-searching, I know the answer: It changed everything because it needed to. I needed to change everything, and somehow the good Lord knew I wasn't going to do it on my own initiative, so He went ahead and did it for me. I needed to change how I lived my life in so many ways if I was going to survive it and have the opportunity to thrive in it. The repeated self-abandonment that was modeled for me, the constant deferring of my opinions, my thoughts, and my feelings, right down to my safety to others who I mistakenly believed knew better than me, were just a few. The meaning I derived from understanding I had not been in the wrong place at the wrong time, but rather, I had been taken out to the desert to learn profound lessons from my Creator about the heart and soul of the human experience, and what I needed to change to deepen my relationship with myself, was so perfectly timed. I am grateful that I did not miss out on the lesson of that blessing. I now understand what it means, and while it took a lot of digging, and I quite literally thought that digging was going to kill me, I'm grateful I did what needed to be done to be here, sharing those lessons learned with you.

To figure out what it all means for us moving forward, we need to understand what it all meant in the first place. Please do not mistake this concept for one of condemnation or blame. I am not suggesting in any way that the kidnapping was my fault, or that if you end up with cancer it was because you didn't eat well enough, or that if you lose a loved one in the battle for their mental health it was because you didn't do enough to save them. What I am suggesting is that we look critically at the habits, practices, and beliefs that have created an ecosystem for which we get caught up while just going about our business and living life. We are often not the chooser of our circumstances, that is for sure, but we are in complete control of our healing journeys and the direction we allow those circumstances to take us.

Survivor Spotlight: Martin Lockett's Reasons for Purpose

I want to tell you a story about a friend of mine, Martin Lockett. Martin is a speaker, author, substance abuse counselor, and advocate for sobriety. His story is a perfect example of turning tragedy into triumph. I got to know Martin because we were both on a popular podcast in separate interviews. After both our interviews aired, Martin reached out to me to connect, and we hit it off, bonding over our life-changing tragedies and the fight to survive survival.

When Martin (who is now in his mid-forties like me) was twenty-four, he made a decision that changed not only the course of his life but the lives of others he didn't even know. A self-described functional alcoholic, Martin had been raised in a loving family but steadily came to rely on alcohol to deal with his mounting anxiety and low self-esteem as a teenager and young adult. He was doing considerably well—living with his girlfriend, going to nursing school, and paying his bills, hence the functional side. On New Year's Eve a little over twenty years ago, Martin got behind the wheel of his car and decided to drive drunk. He ended up causing a horrific car crash in which the driver and passenger of the other car he hit, lost their lives. Martin pled guilty and, as a result, was sentenced to serve twenty years in prison to pay for his crime. Martin talks openly about the depths of despair and self-loathing he experienced in those days following the crash.

As with many who experience significant trauma, Martin had a life-changing moment, just a few days after the event while he was in jail. He tells the story of receiving a newspaper while he was awaiting trial. As he flipped through the pages of the paper, his attention landed on his mugshot next to the picture and write-up of his victims. Ironically, both the deceased individuals were heavily involved in the substance recovery community and had been sober for many years. It was the final line of the article that changed the direction of Martin's life when he read, "Perhaps the person they will have helped the most, is the man who took their lives." It would take Martin weeks, months, and years to settle into life in prison, but he made a very conscious decision that he was going to make a difference and contribute through the practice of service, even while behind bars.

For the next two decades, all while incarcerated, Martin would go on to earn his bachelor's and master's degrees, and in his efforts to make lifelong amends, he reestablished his spiritual roots and grew in his mind and spirit. Martin learned more about his addiction, as he began to unravel the origin story around it, he started a mentor substance abuse program for his fellow inmates. He attended DUI panels, spoke on behalf of the victims' families, and shared his story with full honesty, owning his responsibility for the tragedy he caused, but also establishing a greater purpose and personal mission as a way to honor his victims' legacy. He became a state-certified substance abuse counselor, which allows him to counsel people today.

In our most recent conversation, Martin shared his service view of making meaning out of our life's most challenging moments and turning them into contributions. His belief is that sharing what we have and putting service at the forefront of our purpose makes the healing journey easier because it gives us something to live for. He believes that no one is immune from adversity, and if we spend all our time and energy focused on the hard stuff, we will miss the opportunities for growth and service. "We cannot let our tragedies be in vain," he told me. One of the most profound offerings he left me with was that oftentimes, there isn't a reason for the bad things that happen to us, but that doesn't mean we can't derive purpose from them. My eyes welled up with tears when he said that to me over Zoom. It perfectly articulates how I feel about what I have been through, and what I want people to derive from this book.

Now released from prison, Martin continues his mission and message by helping those in need of counseling for mental health and substance use disorders while sharing his powerful story at DUI victim impact panels, high schools, conferences, and highway safety classes across the country. Martin has survived many things, including the surviving of survival. I am constantly inspired by his commitment to living life, self-forgiveness, and mining the meaning from a chapter in the story of his life. It takes tremendous strength and self-acceptance not to let the most challenging moments be just one chapter of our story and not the entire book. Martin is one of those rare people who has chosen to build his platform while he was in prison, but he has undoubtedly continued to free himself and others as he continues to create meaningful contributions to the world.

* * *

Your past doesn't have to define you, but it can refine you, and Martin is a perfect example of how this is true. He has not allowed his mistakes and subsequent hardships to determine who he is or what he can become. However, those experiences have shaped him, strengthened him, and made him wiser, and he has used the lessons he has learned through those experiences to support and help other people.

Your past doesn't have to define you because your previous choices, circumstances, or struggles do not permanently bind you. Growth, change, and transformation are always possible, but only if you want that transformation. It may not feel like it right now, but the energy you put into who you are in the present moment and who you want to become in the future matters more than who or where you have been.

Consider what your difficult experiences have taught you; are you more resilient? Are you wiser than you were before? Do you have more self-awareness now after all you have survived? All these valuable character traits will help you in so many ways, but especially as you move forward with your life and continue to make choices that will help you with rebuilding that life and trusting your future decision-making. One of my favorite quotes says that challenges don't form character in us but reveal our character. Think about who you are now compared to before the event. It may take a long time to be able to see that—I know for me, it sure did—but it will be illuminated if you are patient and keep showing up. And allow it the time it needs to take.

Instead of seeing your past as a fixed label, think of it as raw material that, when refined, makes you more resilient, insightful, and capable.

How Martin's Story Reflects the RISE Framework

Martin's story is a testament to the idea that even the most devastating mistakes can be transformed into purpose—if we're willing to do the deep work. His journey is not about redemption through perfection, but about responsibility, repair, and choosing to become someone new. The **RISE Framework** lives in every stage of Martin's story, from the moment his life changed forever to the lasting legacy he's now creating in service to others.

R - Reckon with the Pain

The night Martin chose to drive under the influence changed everything—not only for the victims he tragically killed but for everyone connected to that moment. When the full weight of his actions came into focus, Martin didn't run. In the silence of his prison cell, he sat with the unbearable truth of what he had done. He didn't deflect, deny, or distract. He reckoned with the pain of the lives lost and the lives forever altered—including his own. He knew he couldn't undo what had happened, but he could decide what came next.

I - Identify the Impact

Martin began to trace the patterns that led him to that night—how addiction, shame, and the need to belong had shaped so many of his choices. He examined how the pain he carried long before the crash had contributed to his behavior, and he chose to do the work to understand himself from the inside out. Instead of seeing prison as an ending, he saw it as a place to begin again. He took full accountability for the ripple effects of his actions, not just externally, but internally. This wasn't just punishment—it was a process of profound transformation.

S – Seek the Meaning

Martin's moment of clarity came when he read about the lives of the two people he had killed. In an unexpected act of grace, he learned that their families had dedicated themselves to forgiveness and DUI prevention. In that moment, something shifted. He thought, "Maybe the person they helped the most … is the man who took their lives." That line became a seed of purpose. Meaning didn't erase the guilt—but it gave it somewhere to go. He enrolled in college courses, earned two degrees, began mentoring fellow inmates, and started speaking out about addiction and accountability.

E – Embody the Purpose

Today, Martin Lockett is free—and he is using that freedom to serve. He is a public speaker, author, and recovery advocate who shares his story to prevent others from making the same mistake. He works with people struggling with addiction, with youth at risk, and with communities impacted by trauma. He doesn't hide from his past. Instead, he lets it fuel the way he shows up in the world. His story reminds us that even the worst chapter of your life doesn't have to be the last—and that the legacy we leave is shaped by what we do *after* the reckoning.

PAUSE, PONDER, AND PROCESS

We can only **mine the meaning** of our life's hardest moments if we are willing to dig deep into those experiences to extract valuable lessons and wisdom to add to our personal growth. Just as miners search through layers of rock to find precious gems or metals, we must sift through our struggles, pain, and challenges to uncover insights that can enrich our lives.

Steps for Looking Beyond the Surface
What is the more profound significance of your painful experience? Do you believe there is a more profound significance? Why or why not? If you do believe there could be, but you aren't sure how to unearth it, the following steps have been constructive for me in mining the meaning of my experiences.

1. **Try to be the observer instead of the experiencer**
    If you were looking at this experience from an outside perspective, or this had happened to someone else, do you think you would find deeper meaning in it all?

2. **Go deep**
    What has this experience revealed about me—my strengths, weaknesses, values, or fears?

    How has this pain shaped or refined me as a person?

    What could this teach me about life, relationships, resilience, or purpose?

3. **Look for the reframe**
   Try to write about what you are going through by reframing it using the following for context:
   - This was painful, but it also taught me something valuable.
   - This experience changed me—how can I make that change meaningful for myself and others?
   - What if this struggle is preparing me for something greater?
   - How does that make you feel?

4. **Find the pattern that is ready to be put to rest**
   Can you connect this pain to past experiences? If so, write about them.

   Do similar struggles keep showing up in your life? Write about the hardship and see if you can connect the dots.

   What could these patterns be revealing about your choices, beliefs, or personal growth areas? What needs to be changed and what do you need to do in order to change them.

5. **Look for the light**
   Is there light coming in from any place in this situation? Make a list of all the places you could see this as an opportunity for growth.

   Mining the meaning from our hardships is not about denying or glorifying suffering, but rather making sense of it in a way that fuels resilience and deeper meaning in life. A client of mine once told me during a coaching session, "If you focus on the wound, you continue to hurt. If you focus on the lesson, you'll continue to grow . . . and if you focus on the opportunity, nothing from your hardship goes to waste."

   I completely agree.

RISE Reminders

- I don't have to pretend it didn't hurt.
  - The truth doesn't destroy me—it sets me free.
  - I can be honest about what I've lost, and still hold hope.
  - My regret doesn't make me unworthy of healing.
- I am not the same person I was—and that is something to honor.
- My past has shaped me, but it doesn't have to own me.
  - I am not here to stay stuck in shame—I am here to rise.
  - My story can be a lesson, not just a wound.
- My life is a chance to honor the people I've lost—and the person I've become.
  - The legacy I leave can be one of redemption, not regret.

CHAPTER 6
WHO WE BECOME

For those who have survived trauma, loss, or significant life disruption, there often comes a strange and quiet moment—a space after the initial survival, where the question arises: *Who am I now?*

This moment is not about immediate healing or urgent recovery. It's not about putting things back together quickly. Instead, it's the beginning of something deeper: a quiet, aching curiosity that is felt by a need to explore. We know the details of the event, so it's not an excavation of what happened that is essential to our healing journey: it's being open to the truth and able to identify and articulate what has changed in us.

When trauma or loss tears through our lives, it often takes more than just people or circumstances away from us. It can dismantle the very identity we once held and the roles we played. The dreams we had are gone in an instant, taking with them the version of ourselves we once knew. And so, what's left in its wake is not just pain, but a deep, unsettling unfamiliarity. We no longer recognize ourselves.

The Identity Shatter

Psychologists call this phenomenon a *shattered self-concept*. According to a study published in the *Journal of Traumatic Stress* in 1992, trauma often disrupts our core assumptions—about the world, about safety, and about who we are. We might lose the sense of being capable, lovable, or in control. The identity we wore like a second skin suddenly no longer fits. In fact, it may no longer exist.

I remember, early on in my healing journey, I was able to articulate to my therapist that one of my great griefs in this whole ordeal was that my belief in the world being a safe place had been shattered. I had learned in a very strange and extreme way that the world "out there" can be a rough classroom, and I had gotten my ass kicked. In retrospect, I can understand that indeed, I am lucky to have made it that far in life holding onto that belief. Call it naivety, the ignorance of youth, or just being in love with the world, but I had experienced incredible things because I believed the world was a good place and that I was somehow safe in it. The kidnapping destroyed that sense of safety and while I am very proud to say that I can move through my life with a sense of trust now, it has taken me a very long time and a lot of hard work to patch that trust back into place.

For me, the evolution began with understanding that my world had changed, as well as who I was in it. At times, it was heartbreaking and terrifying work, but I wanted to discover who I might become instead.

Curiosity as a Tool for Rebuilding

When we become curious about ourselves after trauma, we begin to shift out of survival mode. Curiosity is a gentle invitation to look at our inner world with less judgment and more wonder. Rather than asking, "What's wrong with me?" we begin to ask, "What happened to me?" and eventually, "What is trying to emerge in me now?"

Research supports this shift. A 2020 study from UCLA found that cultivating curiosity activates brain regions associated with learning, memory, and motivation. It also helps regulate emotional reactivity—a key factor in posttraumatic growth. In other words, curiosity doesn't just feel better. It *changes* our brain.

It's also important to note that curiosity is a *choice*. It's not always easy, and it doesn't always come naturally after trauma. But it is a practice; one that allows us to explore new values, passions, relationships, and identities with openness rather than fear.

The Science of Posttraumatic Growth

Psychologists Tedeschi and Calhoun introduced the concept of posttraumatic growth (PTG), the positive psychological change experienced as a result of the struggle with highly challenging life circumstances. PTG isn't guaranteed—it requires intentional reflection, time, and often support—but it is very real.

Their research highlights five domains where growth can occur:

1. Greater appreciation for life
2. Improved relationships with others
3. Increased personal strength
4. New possibilities in life
5. Spiritual or existential change

What do all these areas have in common? They require exploration. They demand that we ask new questions and invite us in to stretch beyond who we were, and become willing to meet the unfamiliar.

In a long-term study of trauma survivors led by psychologists Stephen Joseph and P. Alex Linley, researchers found that those who engaged in meaning-making activities, such as journaling, therapy, creative expression, or philosophical inquiry, reported significantly higher levels of posttraumatic growth than those who did not.

From Survival to Sovereignty

In the early days of survival, we do what we must to endure. We cope, we compartmentalize, we protect ourselves. And this is valid and necessary. But evolution comes when we begin to move beyond coping into creating.

This is the shift from surviving to reclaiming.

We may begin to ask:

- What do I believe now?
- What do I want to rebuild—and what will I leave behind?
- Who am I becoming?

These questions are not always answered immediately. They are lived. And often, they are lived through trial and error, through trying on new beliefs, relationships, careers, or expressions, and seeing what resonates.

This is not about constructing a new persona. It's about uncovering the truest parts of ourselves that may have been buried—or even born—in the ashes of what we lost.

Exploration as an Act of Power

To explore after trauma is to reclaim your agency. It is to say: I am not only what happened to me. I am what I choose to become next.

That might look like taking a solo trip for the first time. Signing up for a class in something you've always been curious about. Starting a journal. Speaking your story out loud. Trying therapy. Starting a new relationship—or ending one.

Every act of exploration becomes a step toward identity reconstruction. And with each step, the past begins to shape you less—and inform you more.

We do not have to explore alone. In fact, sharing your evolving story with trusted people can accelerate the process. As Brené Brown notes, "When we deny the story, it defines us. When we own the story, we can write a brave new ending."

Storytelling is not just expression; it's integration. And when others witness your story with compassion, they reflect parts of you that you may have forgotten.

Support groups, therapy spaces, artistic communities, and even social media platforms (when used mindfully) can become mirrors. They remind us we're not alone and that there is life after what broke us.

Perhaps the most liberating truth is this: identity is not fixed. We are allowed to evolve—we are meant to. Your story isn't over when the trauma ends, it's being rewritten with every brave, curious step you take toward who you are becoming. You are allowed to outgrow the roles you played in order to survive. You are allowed to become someone new; someone freer, deeper, more aligned.

The Small Moments of Becoming: A Scene from *Room*

There's a beautiful and understated moment in the final scene of the film *Room* (2015), where Brie Larson's character Joy sits with her son in a diner. She's eating a hamburger. After years of captivity and trauma, now free and slowly reentering the world, she pauses mid-bite and says softly, "I don't even know if I like this."

It's such a small thing. A hamburger. It's a passing line, but in that moment, it captures what so many survivors experience: the slow, strange work of rediscovering who they are.

Joy isn't just talking about food. She's speaking to identity. She's realizing that her preferences, her pleasures, and her sense of self might not be what they once were—and that she has the space now to find out.

The healing journey is often made in moments just like this: not grand declarations, but quiet reckonings. She's learning that healing isn't about going back, but rather about discovering what's true now. What fits and what she wants. She is ready to accept who she is becoming.

This scene reminds us that transformation doesn't always roar. Sometimes it whispers, "I'm not sure anymore." And that uncertainty is not a weakness. It's the beginning of curiosity which always leads to freedom.

Survivor Spotlight: Pat Greenwood—Learning to Hear the Whispers

Pat Greenwood says his life's theme is "running face-first into brick walls." And he doesn't mean that metaphorically.

Growing up, he always knew he wanted to serve in the military. He wasn't particular about the branch—he just knew he was built for the fight. By January 2013, he had secured a Special Forces contract and became a Green Beret. Combat wasn't a possibility. It was his primary goal.

For over eight years, Pat lived and breathed the intensity of Special Forces life. He served for a total of eleven years and two months. His only deployment was to Syria, but it left a mark far beyond a single set of orders. The tragic truth of serving our country is that within a span of just a few days, comrades can be lost, which was the case with Pat. He lost four fellow service members, all in varying roles and places, within the span of just a few days. The grief was immediate, but there was no time to process.

"We all had PTSD," Pat says now. "But no one talked about it."

The training for their mission went on, and so did he.

By the time 2020 came, he was back in the States—posted to Fort Belvoir just as the COVID pandemic was turning the world inside out. Even though he was technically "home," he might as well have still been deployed because he was gone constantly, missing family life, missing rest, missing himself.

Then, in April 2021, life gave him something he hadn't had in a long time: space.

He took leave and had a glorious month of quality time with his wife and daughter—it was the first real pause he'd had in years.

But just two days before his daughter's third birthday, the real brick wall found him.

He was riding his motorcycle, just two miles from home; he had the green light. A teenager in the turn lane thought he could make it in time, but misjudged the distance—and hit Pat head-on. In the seconds that followed, Pat's entire face was shattered. He flew off his bike, over the hood and roof of the car, and landed face first on the car's rear windshield. As a result, every single bone in his skull was broken except for his left cheekbone. The impact caused what doctors call a Le Forte III fracture, otherwise known as a complete craniofacial dysjunction—a rare and severe injury that quite literally disconnects the bones of the face from the rest of the skull.

He lost consciousness for nearly an hour and would later learn that he came terrifyingly close to not surviving at all.

But he did. And when he woke up, it wasn't just his face and outward identity that had to be rebuilt. It was his sense of self.

After surviving so much in the military—combat, loss, invisible injuries, emotional isolation—he never imagined it would be a motorcycle accident two miles from home that would force him to reconsider everything. But in that slow, painful, neurologically disorienting recovery, Pat heard something new; it wasn't the roar of combat or the silent grief of losing teammates, but it was the whisper of his life asking for something more.

"That was literally my brick wall," he says. "That accident was God, the Universe—whatever you want to call it—saying, 'You need to stop running and gunning. You need to stay. To live. For your family.'"

With lingering traumatic brain injuries, constant double vision, and a fractured sense of who he used to be, Pat began the long process of rebuilding—not just his neural pathways, but his perspective.

He grieved the loss of his physical capability, the sharpness he once relied on, the identity he carried as a Green Beret. But over time, the grief softened into a new question: *What does it mean to hunt the bad guys now?*

For Pat, purpose didn't disappear after survival, although it changed shape. He realized he could still serve, but maybe not with boots on the ground. Now, he's leaning into cybersecurity and learning how to transfer his discipline, intuition, and tactical mindset into digital defense.

"You don't get to do the last-hardest thing just because you decide to do it," Pat told me. "It's the little things we've survived. The little resiliencies we've built. That's what gives us the foundation to survive survival."

His story is a living map of what it looks like to lose everything you once built your life around—and still rise.

Because, as Pat says, "If we can't run from our pain, we have to lean into it. We have no other choice."

How Pat's Story Reflects the RISE Framework

Pat's story is a powerful example of how surviving survival doesn't always happen in the wake of war. Sometimes, it begins in the stillness after the storm—when everything finally slows down, and the pain that's been following you catches up.

R – Reckon with the Pain

Pat didn't have the luxury of processing grief while deployed. The deaths of four teammates—one a close friend, another their team leader—hit his unit hard, but there was no pause button. Everyone kept moving, carrying silent PTSD beneath the armor.

It wasn't until he hit his own literal and metaphorical brick wall—his near-fatal motorcycle accident—that he was forced to stop running and begin facing the pain he had long avoided.

The physical trauma cracked him open, but so did the emotional reckoning of everything he had pushed down for years.

I – Identify the Impact

The accident didn't just injure his body—it fractured his identity. With lingering traumatic brain injuries, cognitive fog, and constant double vision, Pat had to face what it meant to no longer be the Green Beret he had worked so hard to become. He had to reckon with the mental shift from being someone on the front lines to someone healing in the shadows. He grieved what he had lost—both in the field and in himself—and began the difficult work of asking: *Who am I now?*

S – Seek the Meaning

In the aftermath, Pat didn't try to "get back" to who he was. Instead, he started looking for a new version of service—one that still aligned with his skills and calling, but fit the reality of his life postinjury. He realized that his survival had meaning, and that his ability to endure pain, loss, and recovery had shaped him into someone who could still fight the good fight—just in a different way. He now channels his purpose into cyber defense, protecting others in a new domain with the same conviction that once drove him on the battlefield.

E – Embody the Purpose

Pat's story reminds us that resilience is not forged in comfort, but in repetition. Now, Pat uses his story to speak to others in the military community about grief, transition, and the value of slowing down. He's building a new legacy—one built not just on strength, but on softness, self-awareness, and showing others that it's possible to rebuild a meaningful life, even after everything changes.

PAUSE, PONDER, AND PROCESS

1. What parts of my identity were shaped by my trauma?

2. What have I learned about myself that I didn't know before?

3. What values or desires are emerging now?

4. How can I explore these new parts of myself with curiosity and compassion?

Exploring Who You Are Now

The self that survives is not the same as the one that lived before. And that is not a tragedy. It's a transformation.

Explore who you are becoming. There is wisdom in your wounds—and a new world waiting on the other side of curiosity.

WRITING PROMPTS FOR IDENTITY AFTER TRAUMA

1. **The Present Moment**
   - *Right now, I feel most like myself when . . .*

   - *The parts of me that feel most alive lately are . . .*

   - *If I were to describe myself today as a landscape, I would be . . . (and why?)*

2. **Shedding the Old**
   - *What parts of me no longer fit—roles, beliefs, or stories I used to tell about myself?*

   - *I used to believe _____. Now, I'm beginning to believe _____.*

   - *I survived by being _____. I am learning to live by being _____.*

3. **Embracing the New**
   - *What new desires, values, or dreams are beginning to emerge in me?*

   - *What does the word "freedom" look like in my life now?*

   - *What am I curious about exploring—even if I'm not sure where it will lead?*

4. **Identity in Transition**
   - *If I weren't afraid of what others thought, I would . . .*

   - *What kind of person am I becoming? Describe them in detail—their energy, their habits, their presence.*

   - *I don't fully recognize myself yet in _____, and that's okay because . . .*

5. **Reclaiming Voice and Power**
   - *What do I want to say that I've never said out loud?*

   - *If I could write a letter to the world about who I am now, it would say . . .*

   - *The power I hold now that I didn't before is . . .*

6. **Gratitude and Growth**
   - *Even in the aftermath, I am grateful for . . .*

   - *Something beautiful I've discovered about myself through all of this is . . .*

   - *My pain taught me _____. My healing is teaching me _____.*

   Bonus Prompt: Meet Your Evolving Self
   Write a conversation between your old self (before the trauma/loss) and your emerging self (the version of you now). What do they say to each other? What do they forgive? What do they celebrate?

RISE Reminders

- I can grieve who I was without rushing to become someone new.
- The parts of me that no longer fit aren't failures—they're evidence of growth.
- Curiosity is a quiet form of courage, and it will lead me forward.
- I don't have to return to who I was; I get to rise into who I'm becoming.

CHAPTER 7
THE GREAT INVITATION

The place God calls you to is the place where your deep gladness and the world's hunger meet.
—Frederick Buechner

Purpose: The reason for which something is done or created or for which something exists.[2]

I remember the first time purpose found me. I was prostrate on my college dorm bedroom floor, overcome with empathetic grief over the plight of child soldiers in East Africa. I was just an aspiring schoolteacher who had grown up in the middle of a cornfield in Ohio. Still, through a series of heartbreaking personal events, I enrolled in college again, this time far away from home, so that I could start my life over. It didn't take long for me to latch on to

2   *Oxford English Dictionary*, "purpose (n.)," June 2025, https://doi.org/10.1093/OED/1711703121.

the idea that there was a big, wide world out there to discover, and I believed so many people needed help. Really, and indeed, that became my goal and the thing I connected with in the wee hours of the morning. Whether I was up late, studying for finals or working four summer jobs so I could pay for my education classes, it was my belief in doing something greater that motivated me to keep going. I had a purpose and was driven to reach my goal of going to Africa to teach. That dream led me to a serendipitous meeting with a woman named Rosemarie one winter day at a school-sponsored conference in Kentucky. She was a teacher at an international school in Nairobi, Kenya, and we connected on such a soul level. It was as if she had been waiting there for me, just to tell me about The Rosslyn Academy in Nairobi, and I'm pretty sure she was, because the next year, I was there, teaching alongside her as a student teacher. The school offered me a full-time position as a classroom teacher for fourth grade, and I happily accepted!

Fast forward a few months, when I met my husband Erik on a dance floor in a trashy night club (to read the complete account of how "Orik" and I met that night, you'll have to read our *NYT* bestseller, *Impossible Odds*!) and a few years later, I had gotten even closer to my dream of working with child soldiers, when I was hired to be the regional education advisor for the Danish Demining Group to develop materials and train staff on mine risk education, firearm safety, conflict management, and armed violence reduction. While living and working in Somaliland, based in Hargeisa with most expats who lived and worked in the Horn of Africa, that fateful trip down south to Galkayo would change my purpose-driven life.

While there was so much to process and so many complex emotions, truths, and untruths to wade through as I moved through my emotional healing, one of the most challenging ideas to reconcile was this belief I carried that my purpose had shriveled up and died out in the desert. I tried hard to resurrect it by going back to work for my NGO after taking a few months off. But no matter how much effort I put into giving my old job another chance, my heart wasn't in it anymore, even though I had loved it so much. Part of the problem was the aftereffects of the general trauma that I reexperienced every time I pulled out my computer to work. I had been given a desk to work at in the regional office in Nairobi so as not to have to return to the field. Still, it wasn't long before panic attacks and overwhelming bouts of anxiety would make it impossible for me to even turn on my computer. I couldn't concentrate on the tasks at hand, I couldn't produce creative ideas the way I used to, and when my supervisor told me I was going to have to go back to fieldwork again, it didn't take me very long to decide it was time to quit. I can imagine that is exactly what they wanted me to do, but that is neither here nor there anymore.

Erik and I decided to leave everything we had built and the life we loved in Kenya behind and start a new life in the US. It was harder than we both thought it was going to be, but for Erik, as a native Swede, he was still living abroad as an expat. It was new and exotic for him. I felt like things had come full circle, but not in the direction that I had planned, imagined, or wanted.

As we settled into building our new lives, the necessary act of reinventing ourselves became our first order of business. It wasn't hard for Erik, as we planted roots in the DC area. Many people worked in the international development industry, and he quickly made connections and found work. But for me, well, I was lost. I couldn't picture going back to the classroom, and outside of field-work, I knew I would never fit in well in the corporate DC environment, even if I did work on similar content for another international nongovernmental organization. I would sit on the sofa for hours, combing through LinkedIn and professional websites, desperately trying to glean any direction to move forward. I paid hundreds, if not thousands, of dollars for professional evaluations that told me I would make an excellent teacher and public speaker—both of which I knew already! I cannot describe my frustration with myself and our situation and that I could not figure out what to do with my life. In some of the darkest moments of this metamorphosis, I wondered why I had even survived if there was nothing for me to do or contribute to the world.

* * *

I put a lot of pressure on myself in general. This has always been my personality—I grew up with a critical mother and was confined within the boundaries of a very controlling form of organized religion. I am also the oldest of three, to which I became somewhat of a caretaker of my siblings when my mother's mental illness took her away from us for a couple of years. I often felt like the weight of the world, and other people's experiences in that world, were my responsibility to fix or create, even at ten years old. So, it was a familiar feeling, this weight, when I became the girl rescued by SEAL Team Six; it was the new albatross around my neck.

No one told me I needed to carry that around the way I did, least of all these fantastic soldiers, but I felt so indebted to them for putting their lives on the line for little old me. When I found out the amount of work and resources that had gone into rescuing me, all the way up the chain of command to the sitting president of the United States—that was almost more than I could fathom, and I felt this tremendous sense of responsibility to do something incredible to pay it forward and let them know how grateful I was to be alive, not just the SEALs, but my entire country. I needed to prove to them that I was worth saving. What an exhausting and fruitless hill to climb!

It would require extensive exploration, many years of growth, and significant trial and error for me to love myself and believe that my purpose hadn't faded away in the desert. Just because I couldn't cure cancer or become the CEO of an international nongovernmental organization didn't mean I didn't have something meaningful to glean from my experiences, to transform the horror of it into contributions that could help someone out there who was struggling.

* * *

I can't say I really planned it; rather, I settled into following my intuition. One winter evening, I was out on a date with my husband—which was a rarity—at twenty dollars an hour for a babysitter for both kids, we didn't get out a lot! I was feeling deeply depressed and frustrated about my lack of direction, and Erik, the person who probably knows me best in the whole world, called me out on it. We had been sitting in the same place, having the same conversation, on another winter evening almost precisely a year before, and nothing had changed, except perhaps my happiness level had gone from a six to a three in the year that had passed.

Erik took a sip of his California red and pinned me to my chair with his knowing gaze. "Jess, what do you want to do with your life?" he asked.

Tears pricked the inside of my eyelids as I nervously scanned the wine bar we were sitting in. I had no answer to this all-consuming question. I wanted to hurl my wine glass across the room and scream out that I had no idea what to do with my life because I didn't know who I was anymore or what mattered to me. I didn't know what I was passionate about and didn't know if I was qualified to do anything anymore. I had sought help in so many different ways, but couldn't come up with the answer. And it was infuriating. I felt like I had been turned into a freak by circumstances that I did not choose, nor could I control.

That conversation on a snowy night in January was the prompt (or kick in the ass!) that I needed to get quiet and start figuring some things out. I sat down and made a list of the subjects that interested me the most and realized my interest in plants and their medicinal uses, while ignited during my time in Africa, still burned inside me, especially as I tried to approach motherhood more naturally. This led me to years of studying Western Herbalism formally. While I don't necessarily practice that solely today, I learned so much about nature, including how to heal myself emotionally and spiritually through my connection with plants. I also made some wonderful memories and friends along the way. It wasn't where I ended up, but it was a wonderful respite on my long and winding path toward my purpose. It was a stepping stone that I took because it felt interesting. It didn't make much sense, but I have found that the most interesting paths we take in life rarely do.

Even though one of my reasons for pursuing something so entirely and seemingly random as herbalism for a new career path was in search of my purpose, it was not lost on me that I was trying to outrun my testimony. There were times that I outright lied when someone in the class started to put two and two together. I could see the light start to dawn in their eyes when they figured out who I was. I wanted so badly to "start over" and be this random mom who wanted to learn the medicinal uses of garlic and chamomile so my kids would stay healthy. But try as I might, I couldn't stay hidden for too long.

The need to write more started making itself known too, and while early morning writing sessions simply did not fit into my life schedule, I spent many long hours at night in the living room, typing away in the glow of my computer screen after the kids went to bed. Memories and events from the kidnapping, things I was pondering or lessons I was learning in motherhood and healing my PTSD began pouring out of me between the hours of eight p.m. and midnight. As is the case with many budding authors (although I had already published a very successful book), I felt the need for outside support and, if I'm honest, validation. It was through being rejected from a writing group that I was introduced to a woman in my neighborhood who was also experimenting in the memoir space and had been rejected from this same writing group. We hit it off, and I was so relieved to find someone as serious about their writing journey as I was! We formed a group, but on the Saturday afternoon of our first meeting, we were the only ones who showed up. It was at her kitchen table that the idea for a podcast was born. We worked together for over three years, hosting hundreds of conversations, writing thousands of scripts, and reading many great books to pre-pare for author interviews. It was amazing—but as much as I loved having these conversations and working with my partner, a part of me longed to write more and in a different way than podcasting required.

During this time, I started writing my second memoir, *Deserts to Mountaintops*, and got halfway through the manuscript when I realized the world didn't need another memoir from me, or at least that's what I believed. What I felt it needed, however, was a plat-form for other women to share their stories of what they had been through, what they had learned, and the lessons they wanted to share with the world. It had taken me many years and countless journaling sessions to realize the reason I ended up kidnapped was that I had lost my voice—I had been silenced by my organization, which was such a familiar experience, having grown up in the church and in such a strict home, where God's will was what I was taught to seek and hopefully find. As I began to examine and explore these themes in my journals and through microblogging, I realized there were so many women out there who had experienced being victimized in their own lives because they had been silenced in a variety of ways by a variety of people. I didn't know what would happen when I had this idea to build a book-writing project and turn *Deserts to Mountaintops* into an anthology with a coaching component added to it. But I knew I needed to try.

What happened was the birth of my next purpose, and while the path getting there was long, winding, and sometimes unforgiving in its workload, from where I am standing now, I can say it was so worth the climb, because the view is spectacular!

* * *

At the time of this writing, Soul Speak Press came about four years ago due to an epic business failure I was on the heels of wrapping up. I had gone into business with a fellow inspirational speaker who was interested in helping other women grow in their abilities to speak professionally, and while we had a honeymoon phase, it became clear, quite quickly, that we were not aligned and all the work we had done just evaporated into thin air. I was devastated and had no idea what I was going to do next. I spent an entire day completely panicked, and I can still remember the emotional angst I was in as I spent hours driving up and down the George Washington Memorial Parkway, screaming in hysterics about what a mistake I had made and how I had no idea what I was going to do with my life. Once I calmed down, I headed home and found my husband, who was always such a source of stability and comfort in these times of confusion and duress. He listened and handed me a tissue so I could stop wiping my face on my shirt. I was exhausted and thoroughly wrung out, but I will never forget what he said to me: "Jess, you are an entrepreneur. This is the life of the entrepreneur. You are more resilient than this, and you will figure it out."

I took a few more days to feel sorry for myself—and in all honesty, made some not great choices about my alcohol consumption, which resulted in a long night, if you know what I mean. But something about the whole experience, from the emotional to the physical purge, renewed my resolve, and I emerged as a different woman. The next Monday morning, I kid you not! I was committed to my coaching services, and I *knew* I was doing what I was supposed to do; I just hadn't gotten it quite right yet.

Providence knew too, so it is no accident that I ended up on a call with one of my clients to let her know we were going out of business. We were talking through logistics when she mentioned something about participating in an anthology project with a group of women out of Canada, where she was from. It would have been easy to miss, but my spirit was ready to receive that divine guidance. In less than thirty seconds, I had put the plan together with a few follow-up questions—and then it was in my lowest professional moment that my multi-six-figure publishing house for women was born! After years of helping women articulate their stories, walking them through incredibly cathartic and intimate coaching sessions, allowing space for their life lessons to emerge onto the page, and then supporting them through the publishing process, I feel I have finally found a purpose for where I can place my pain. Between my work at Soul Speak Press, and all the speaking I do, talking to people about change, and how it is our proof of life—I know that I am doing purpose driven work that I would never have been able to do had I not gone through what I've gone through. Don't get me wrong, I wouldn't want to go through it again! But now that it's over and I've given things the time they need, to heal and grow, I am grateful for the platform I have built and all the people I get to help.

I am finishing this chapter from the airport, enroute from a speaking event in Jamaica of all places, and I keep thinking about an interaction I had with a gentleman who came up to me last night when I was signing books. After I personalized the front cover, he shook my hand, looked me right in the eye and said, "Jessica, your story has changed my life." I was taken aback. While I receive many compliments after speaking, no one has ever said something so unbelievably kind, and I have never been so humbled. I didn't have the opportunity to hear what was going on with his life right then, but walking to my room last night, exhausted from the adrenaline surge of standing up in front of a group of people, and spent from going back to the trauma in an effort to teach and inspire them, well, it felt sort of worth it.

Figuring out my purpose has felt like a deep exhale after holding my breath for a long time. It's a mix of clarity, relief, and an overwhelming sense of alignment—like I've finally clicked into place after feeling lost or out of sync for so long.

It's not always fireworks and grand revelations. Sometimes, purpose makes itself known through a quiet knowing, a deep inner peace that whispers, *This is it. This is what I was meant to do.* Other times, it's electrifying—like a surge of energy that makes me want to run toward my future without hesitation. I've been lucky enough to experience both of those sensations at different points in my life. The magic comes when you wait, you get quiet, you do the thing, even if you are terrified.

Sometimes I feel like all the struggles, the pain, the detours—they weren't for nothing. I believe they were shaping me, preparing me. When I stand in purpose, either on a stage, or on the other side of a Zoom call holding space for one of my authors, there's a weight that lifts off of me because I no longer have to chase meaning—I *am* the meaning.

And it doesn't mean life gets easy, but it does get *clear*. Swimming in clear water is not any easier than swimming in murky water, but it's a heck of a lot more delightful! The doubts don't disappear entirely, but they don't control me anymore. I wake up early, with direction, even on the hard days. And perhaps the most beautiful part? I have stopped asking, *Why did this have to change everything for me?* and can now confidently say, *I see why this happened for me.*

Survivor Spotlight: Gillian Lichota Rises

Change is an invitation to collaborate on your big life project, or your purpose. We love these stories of the significant pivots. These underdogs have lost everything only to find their way to the top because they highlight the struggle of the human experience, rendering us less lonely. Still, they also highlight the possibilities and the magic of the human experience and what it means to be alive. That may be why I am so obsessed with memoir manifestos and this idea that the hard things we face are meant to teach us lessons we can share.

When I think about turning pain into purpose, my friend Gillian Lichota comes to mind. I met Gillian when she connected with me to work on our third *Deserts to Mountaintops* anthology project

The Pilgrimage of Motherhood. I was immediately drawn to Gillian through her story of being a young woman in the breast cancer community, and the fact that she was living boldly as a terminal cancer patient, even though she carries the diagnosis of stage IV metastatic breast cancer, and will for the rest of her life.

While we were working together to create her chapter on her experience of motherhood, several stories came from her, some we decided to keep on the shelf and off the page, but committed to using for future projects. The inception of her nonprofit, the iRise Above Foundation, was one of them, and a story I am grateful to get to tell now.

In 2012, Gillian Lichota was in the prime of her life and her career: She had fulfilled her lifelong goal of becoming a marine biologist at the National Oceanic and Atmospheric Administration in Washington, DC, and then she married the love of her life and together, they were building a beautiful life of adventure, traveling, and, hopefully, family. When they decided it was time for them to grow their family, IVF treatments were needed, and to Gillian's shock, just a few days after beginning her treatments she noticed a burning pain in her right breast along with a dimple, and then to her dismay, a mass. She assumed it was a side effect of IVF treatment but made an appointment with her doctor, just to be on the safe side. Thrilled when an early test revealed that she was pregnant, she was simultaneously devastated by the results of the ultrasound and biopsy: the mass was malignant. Gillian was diagnosed with stage III advanced, estrogen and progesterone hormone breast cancer, which was being fueled by her pregnancy.

Determined to save their unborn child, Gillian rejected the advice of the first oncologist, who pressed Gillian to terminate the pregnancy and begin chemo immediately. Instead, the couple reached out to friends who are physicians with the Johns Hopkins University system, and those doctors helped them establish their dream team of oncologists and reconstructive surgeons that would remove Gillian's affected breast and protect her unborn child. She underwent surgery to remove her breast just eleven days after she learned she had cancer.

At twenty weeks pregnant, Gillian began chemotherapy. Lying in the chemo suite trying to ignore the stares at her pregnant belly, Gillian felt overwhelmed by her fears, but at the same time she also was determined to heal and take charge of her health and future. When Gillian recounts this traumatic experience, she says, "I had this epiphany while I was sitting there, looking around at all these other cancer patients. 'What if I couldn't do the things I loved anymore? What if this was it? What would I regret? What would I wish that I had done?' I knew this couldn't be the end for me. That was my motivation. It was to do it for myself and all of these women who weren't going to get the opportunity to live."

Gillian delivered her son safely, and then proceeded to receive aggressive chemo, undergo another mastectomy and reconstruction, as well as daily radiation for six weeks. She resolved to celebrate her return to health and fitness by climbing a mountain, but not just any mountain. In her follow-up appointment with her oncologist, she outlined her plan for mountain climbing as a response to all she had been through. Her doctor looked at her with awe and amusement and simply asked: "And where?" Her reply? "I have my heart set on going to Tanzania and climbing Mount Kilimanjaro." She laughs when she tells this part of the story because all her doctor did was stare at her and say, "Well, I'll see you in six months."

On the night of a full moon, after miles and miles of climbing and thousands of feet of altitude changes, Gillian and a close friend reached the summit of Mount Kilimanjaro in time to witness the sunrise over Africa. When asked to share her immediate thoughts about that monumental moment, she said: "The full moon symbolizes rebirth. I saw this whole experience as a big 'F—you' to cancer. I was saying as I stood there on top of that mountain: 'I'm alive and I'm going to do this. I'm going to close that chapter, and I'm going to move forward anew.'"

Gillian did move forward, celebrating the birth of her daughter Laykelyn four years later, in August 2016. Then, a few months after her daughter was born, during a ski trip with friends to celebrate her fortieth birthday, Gillian felt a burning pain in her back and lower rib cage that reminded her of the pain she had felt in her breast. Her doctor wasn't concerned at first, but after reviewing her scans and an additional biopsy, the reality was clear. The cancer had returned and metastasized.

Gillian descended into deep grief.

"I was stuck, ruminating over how limiting that was for my life, instead of determining how to untangle myself from my negative experience and trauma, so that I could shift my perspective and pour myself into a positive way to live with more intention, with more purpose."

As her physicians put a treatment plan together, Gillian constructed a plan of her own. She resolved to be proactive in her healing, putting her scientific training to work by researching alternative treatments to supplement conventional treatment. Her first act was to eliminate the stressors in her life, which meant leaving her dream job. The effect was positive: Her cancer antigen numbers decreased in just a few months before she began conventional treatment. Along with traditional therapies—an oophorectomy and Ibrance—Gillian adopted the recommendations of Dr. Jane McLelland in her book

How to Starve Cancer. Eight months after Gillian began following Dr. McLellan's protocol, her scans showed no sign of the tumors, and her breast cancer antigen number was the lowest it had ever been. To date, there is no evidence of disease, so she is termed "stable." And so, she moved on from just sheer survival, to that space of surviving survival. Even as Gillian healed physically and emotionally, she felt alone and cast adrift. Despite the outstanding conventional care that she received, she was frustrated by the lack of targeted, age-appropriate resources for young women like her who were struggling with issues that traditional treatment neglected due to this being a postmenopausal disease, like self-image, relationships, intimacy, and mental and emotional well-being—all elements of life that are important and central to young people.

Gillian was also troubled by the disempowering messages that focused on survivorship, leaving young women with breast cancer feeling like victims. Still other messages urged these women to return to "normal life" after treatment, even though life-altering side effects and the trauma of breast cancer irrevocably changed them. Her own experience showed her that addressing mental health challenges was every bit as crucial and challenging as treating cancer. She needed to get to the root of her dis-ease.

Combined with realizing other young women were experiencing the same sense of isolation, Gillian received another epiphany. "I was determined to fill the gaps I experienced, live my best life, and change the conversation about breast cancer, particularly as it relates to young women like me," Gillian says.

In 2017, Gillian established the iRise Above Foundation to help other women like her to do the same thing: to self-advocate and not rely solely on their oncologist to drive their treatment. She wanted to establish an organization that provided women with information and tools about the myriad of treatment modalities they can incorporate into their lives so they may move from surviving into thriving. And she wanted to build a community of like-minded women who wanted to ditch limiting beliefs and do more than survive.

iRise Above Foundation offers a variety of ways for women of all stages who are living with breast cancer in their twenties, thirties, and forties to connect more deeply with themselves, each other, and the world around them. They offer in person and virtual wellness programs, as well as informative workshops and webinars and retreats. And what I find most amazing, specially organized adventure trips! The iRise Above Foundation recognizes that for women to find their whole self post-breast cancer diagnosis they need support and avenues to explore who they now are—their organization exists to help women reclaim their power and be the authors and creators of their own respective stories. Gillian says, "Many young women want to lead with open-hearted curiosity and explore. With that gift comes a world filled with heart-bursting possibilities and fulfillment—hope for a brighter future, richer with intention, passion, and purpose. Part of healing and living well after breast cancer is connecting with nature while feeling inspired and empowered to live a great story."

As another sort of survivor, I couldn't agree more. To date, Gillian's organization has presented virtual workshops and webinars to over 3000 participants, held book clubs for over 150 women, held in-person and virtual wellness programs for well over 700 women, and has facilitated adventure trips and restorative retreats for over 100 women who have navigated the rocky terrain of breast cancer. They have been all over the globe: Patagonia, Peru, Costa Rica, Mexico, Nepal, Canada, and Utah. Each year, iRise Above raises at least $75,000 to support these women who are not just survivors, but thrivers.

How Gillian's Story Reflects the RISE Framework
R – Reckon with the Pain

Gillian's diagnosis came at what should have been the most joyful time in her life—pregnancy. Instead, she was faced with a decision no one should ever have to make: fight for her own life or protect the one growing inside her. She chose both. That decision began her reckoning—not only with her cancer but with the fear, grief, and limitations it introduced. Later, when the cancer returned and metastasized, Gillian spiraled into despair again, but she didn't stay there. She gave herself time to grieve fully, then faced her new reality with fierce determination.

I – Identify the Impact

Her career, her health, her expectations for the future—all were profoundly altered. And yet, Gillian began to see that her experience gave her something else: a perspective and urgency that others might not have. The pain didn't just strip away her sense of safety—it exposed what mattered most. She identified that beyond her role as a patient or survivor, she was a leader, a researcher, and a woman with insight that could help others.

S – Seek the Meaning

Instead of seeing her illness as the end of her purpose, Gillian saw it as the beginning of a new one. She asked hard questions: What would I regret? What do I wish I had done? The answers led her to summit Kilimanjaro and, ultimately, to establish the iRise Above Foundation. She turned the trauma of her diagnosis and recurrence into a source of meaning—for herself and for the hundreds of young women she now supports.

E – Embody the Purpose

Gillian didn't stop at healing herself—she created a platform for others to thrive. Through retreats, webinars, and outdoor adventure programs, she's helping women with breast cancer rediscover their vitality and power. She built a legacy rooted in choice, empowerment, and community. Her story proves that purpose doesn't have to be postponed until after survival—it can be the engine that carries us through it.

Purpose Is the Key to Your Mental Health

According to The National Library of Medicine, "Some research indicates that purpose in life may build greater resilience after exposure to negative events."[3] The study goes on to propose that "purpose in life predicts both health and longevity, suggesting that the ability to find meaning from life's experiences, especially when confronting life's challenges, may be a mechanism underlying resilience. Having purpose in life may motivate reframing stressful situations to deal with them more productively, thereby facilitating recovery from stress and trauma."[4]

Simply said, having a reason to exist after trauma, in fact, finding purpose in existing *because* of the trauma or hardship is an act of resilience. Assigning meaning to these unspeakably hard things and then looking for a place to plant them as seeds of possibility, even if just for the simple reason to offload them, can still take root and cause personal and community growth.

---

3   "Purpose in Life Can Lead to Less Stress, Better Mental Well-being," American Psychiatric Association, last modified December 7, 2023, https://www.psychiatry.org/news-room/apa-blogs/purpose-in-life-less-stress-better-mental-health.
4   Schaefer, Stacey M et al. "Purpose in Life Predicts Better Emotional Recovery from Negative Stimuli," PLOS One 8, no. 11 (2013): doi:10.1371/journal.pone.0080329.

This can be a slippery slope, for sure. I've seen people throw themselves into the service of others without taking a beat to recover, rest, repair, and heal from trauma—that was a common practice amongst aid workers when I was living and working in East Africa; this kind of reaction is to be expected, especially in hardship posts where there is a job to be done. Many times, we didn't have the opportunity to even stop and realize what we had been through or witnessed, or that we had been traumatized, because we just didn't stop to feel it or process it. If that is your situation, you are not who I am writing this book for (yet!). I am also not suggesting that if you are suffering from depression at any level, in any way, that you are doing so because you have a lack of purpose. Not at all. There are many reasons people experience depression, and as I will continue to remind you, I am not a mental health professional, just a girl who has learned some lessons the hard way and would like to share them with you.

What I do know is that the mind needs something to focus on—it needs a project or a direction, or to be in meditation for twenty-two hours a day, otherwise, it will drive you to the point of no return if you do not give it something to focus on at any given time. When we have no direction, no focus, no goals it can make us feel as if we have no reason to have survived or exist; our thoughts become our beliefs, and so, over time, it is no surprise that we are going to feel depressed. For some, it's easier to lift ourselves out of the valley than it is for others. I watched this firsthand with my mother. She fought tooth and nail, and while she spent many years wandering in the darkness, eventually, she found her way to the light, and I think it was at that point she chose her purpose—which was: her kids, her family, her home. That purpose led her back to us. I know there were moments when she felt so low that she didn't want to live anymore, and she tried more than once to bring that to our reality, but against the odds, she lived, and was able to thrive, despite having a brain that didn't really want to cooperate and massive childhood trauma to wade through. She trained her mind to understand what was real and what was the depression, and she managed, most days, to get out of bed and create a life filled with meaning and purpose within the context of our family. It wasn't easy—but it was possible, and when I start to doubt that, I think about her because she is the proof I need that I have what it takes to pursue purpose and move forward for another day.

* * *

It's well known that trauma changes us fundamentally, not just our ability to process feelings and information, but our brain chemistry as well. Trauma alters the actual structure of our brain, how it functions, and the chemistry that makes everything work the way it was designed to. It's when our nervous system gets stuck in fight-flight-or-freeze mode that can often lead us to feeling a sense of hopelessness and paralyzing fear that can lead us to experiencing depression and anxiety. I spent a long time in this space, and I will be honest when I say it was one of the scariest times of my life, in the aftermath of my kidnapping. I struggled with panic attacks, racing thoughts, debilitating anxiety, bouts of depression and sobbing, as well as nightmares that would wake me up in the middle of the night in full-on terror. I had watched depression steal my mother from us when I was an early adolescent, and I was petrified that the same thing was going to happen to me. I do not want to be too dismissive of this part of my healing journey from depression; but I want to connect my experience to hopefully bring some insight to yours.

When we have found a reason to exist, whether it is through service, art, advocacy, community, education, writing, building, whatever, we are empowered and have a worthwhile reason to get up in the morning because it feels good to exist in a way that isn't just for ourselves, and ourselves alone. The practice of focusing on a message, a body of work, the building of something that can solve a problem someone else might have is incredibly proficient in rewiring our traumatized brains. It takes time, and it is not a one-size-fits-all scenario, but I believe in its efficacy.

Survivor Spotlight: Fran Racioppi—What Do I Have to Do Today to Get to Tomorrow?

For Fran Racioppi, becoming a Green Beret wasn't just a goal—it was the defining dream of his life. From a young age, he was laser-focused on serving at the highest level of military operations. And he didn't just meet that goal—he exceeded it, earning top marks in every position he held, rising through the ranks with unwavering discipline, and earning the kind of respect that can't be requested, only proven.

But the military he gave everything to would ultimately break his heart.

In 2006, while deployed to Iraq, Fran was assaulted by an Iraqi police officer during an offensive operation. The unit investigating the incident made a clerical error in Francis's file—an error that, while minor at the time, would come back with life-altering consequences a decade later.

As Fran prepared to accept a promotion to major—one that was a clear reflection of his leadership and record—he was notified that the promotion was under further review. The reason? That one clerical error. Even though the mistake was widely acknowledged, the system could not (or would not) correct it. His case was reviewed again and again. It was approved by the Secretary of Defense, and even the President, but no resolution ever came from the Senate Armed Services Committee.

Fran had spent his life preparing for leadership, excellence, and honor. But now, he was faced with a painful choice: keep fighting the system that had failed him or walk away from the only dream he had ever known.

He left the army.

He earned his MBA. He took leadership roles at companies like Merrill Lynch, Snapchat, and a cannabis company run by a Russian oligarch, working as the chief security officer. But in a cruel echo of what had happened in the military, each of these roles were ripped from him. A poor fit in finance, an unfounded, defamatory claim at Snapchat, and COVID upheaval in cannabis. He eventually settled a lawsuit, but by then the damage had been done. He was unemployed. He was living with his mother. His name had been dragged through the news multiple times.

Everything he had built time and time again had crumbled.

"I just stood there in the rubble of my life," Fran said, "and asked myself, 'What do I have to do today in order to get to tomorrow?'"

That single question became his turning point. Not all at once—but slowly, intentionally, he began to rebuild.

Even after everything, he still believed the army got it right. Every person he had worked with, every superior, every teammate—had stood behind him. They knew who he was. And so did he.

He realized he hadn't lost his purpose—he had just outgrown the container that once held it.

Fran still believed in service. He still believed in leadership. And he had always believed in the power of stories. Watching the news distort facts, weaponize narratives, and erode public trust lit a new fire in him. He knew what it felt like to be misrepresented. He knew what it cost.

And so, he launched ***The Jedburgh Podcast***, named after the WWII Jedburgh teams—America's original special operations forces. It was more than a podcast. It was a mission: to preserve the values of the Special Forces, to give back to the Green Beret Foundation, and to elevate the voices of rational, courageous, mission-driven leaders in a world increasingly dominated by soundbites and spin.

The show is now viewed over three million times per month. What started from a laptop in his mother's attic has grown into a five-person production team. But more than anything, it's become Fran's personal expression of unfinished service. He didn't find what he was looking for after the army, so he built it himself.

His advice to anyone navigating the uncertain terrain of surviving survival?

"Stay the course. Know your values. Keep preparing today to build your tomorrow. The world may try to take your reputation, your job, even your identity—but your values? Those are yours to protect. Double down on them."

How Fran's Story Reflects the RISE Framework
R – Reckon with the Pain

Fran had to face the deep betrayal of being denied his life's dream—not for performance, but because of bureaucracy. Leaving the army forced him to grieve the loss of identity, purpose, and a community that had shaped him.

I – Identify the Impact

The series of job losses and public defamation shook his confidence, but also revealed his resilience. He was forced to confront how much of his worth he had tied to titles and external validation—and to begin untangling it.

S – Seek the Meaning

Fran realized his story wasn't over—it was evolving. His desire to serve hadn't disappeared, it had just shifted form. He could still lead, still serve, still impact lives—just in a new way.

E – Embody the Purpose

By founding *The Jedburgh Podcast*, Fran reclaimed agency over his narrative and created a platform that gives back, educates, and uplifts. He turned survival into service. Again.

PAUSE, PONDER, AND PROCESS

1. When has a setback forced you to redefine your identity or purpose? What did you learn about yourself in that process?

2. Are there values or missions from your past that still burn within you—but need a new container to grow?

3. What might it look like to "build what you can't find"?

4. **Have you ever been misrepresented or unfairly judged? How did you reclaim your story?**

5. **What do you need to do today to get to the tomorrow you want to build?**

6. **What has life asked you to survive—and what has it revealed in you?**
   Reflect on the hardships you've faced. What strengths, insights, or values have emerged from those experiences?

7. **In what ways has purpose already whispered to you, even if you didn't realize it at the time?**
   Think back to moments of curiosity, fulfillment, or longing. Where have you felt deeply connected or called to something greater?

8. **What limiting beliefs do you still carry about what's possible for you now?**
   Be honest about the stories you tell yourself—about your worth, your capacity, or your future. Whose voice are you listening to? Is it time to change the narrative?

9. **What might your version of "climbing Kiliman-jaro" look like?**
   It doesn't have to be a literal mountain. What bold or symbolic step could represent your commitment to living with purpose?

10. **What would it look like to live not just for yourself, but from yourself?**
    Explore how you might begin to build or express something that flows from your truth, even if it's quiet or unseen by others.

RISE Reminders

- Purpose doesn't always roar—it often arrives as a whisper, inviting us to follow what matters.
- I am not defined by the diagnosis or the detour. I am defined by what I choose to do next.
- It's not selfish to want more than survival. It's sacred.
- When I turn my pain into purpose, I offer others a map—proof that growth is still possible.

CHAPTER 8
YOUR OPTIONS, YOUR CHOICE

Surviving a traumatic experience is no small feat. But as we know, survival alone is not the end of the journey—it is the beginning of a new path that leads us to a different identity, purpose, and a rearranged life. Trauma leaves an imprint on our mind and soul, but it also offers the raw material for transformation, a clean slate, if you will.

I'm a big believer in the difference between options and choices. We often use those words interchangeably but in reality, they do not mean the same thing. According to the dictionary, an option is the "power or right to choose" whereas a choice is "the act of making a decision when two or more possibilities exist."

I was forty or so days into captivity when I realized there was a difference between the two. I woke up at dawn, my body sore and exhausted from my fortieth night spent on the ground. I was drenched in dew, as we were never taken to a house or any kind of structure, we were completely exposed to the elements twenty-four hours a day. Admittedly, I was not in a very good mood when I woke up. I was grumpy and sick of the situation. Poul brought me a cup of oversweet *chai* and I drank it begrudgingly. After I finished what would be my only meal for the day, a piece of bread that had been baked in the sand underneath coals from the cooking fire, I moved my mat from the field to under the acacia tree where I would spend the next twelve hours trying not to go insane.

I was quite the yogi back then and while I still practice yoga today, it's not nearly the same as it used to be. It was impossible to notice how much weight I had lost when moving through my sequences, but as callouses were starting to build up on my rear end, I knew it was very important to keep moving for as long as I could. After I moved through a flow, I settled in at the base of the tree and leaned back to rest, taking great care not to poke myself with the thorns that were growing out of the tree's trunk. I looked out over the vastness of the desert, noticing the beauty of the tall grasses waving in the breeze, the sun was not high enough to be unbearable yet, and I watched its rays shine through the lacy green of the acacia branches. As my mind wandered I had what can only be described as an aha moment or an epiphany. I looked down at the base of the tree and remembered something I had heard from one of my yoga teachers during class. Hadn't the Buddha reached enlightenment while sitting at the base of a tree? (I looked it up after I was rescued, and indeed, he did! He meditated for fifty-nine days at the base of a bodhi tree!) And then I started thinking about my own religious tradition. Having grown up in church in the Midwest, Jesus was very much an integral part of my religious culture. I remembered the stories I had heard in Sunday school during Easter about Jesus wandering the desert for forty days and forty nights, wrestling with his humanity in the face of his impending crucifixion. I looked around and saw the significance and it moved me. The tree, the desert . . . I thought of other spiritual greats and historic icons who had wandered through their own metaphorical (or literal) desert, and I began to draw strength from their stories.

From my perspective, I had three options: I could try to run away, which wasn't viable. I had no idea where I was, and the desert is so hot during the day, I knew I would die out there trying to find my way into town. I figured that the surrounding villages must have been in cahoots with what was happening too, otherwise they wouldn't let us stay in camps outside their towns. My second option was to just end it all. I didn't spend a whole lot of time considering that as a viable option because there is nothing like facing death all day, every day, to make you decide you really want to live.

The third option was the safest, and the most frustrating. I could sit and wait. Wait for a ransom to be paid, wait for them to decide that forty-five million dollars was unrealistic, and wait for whatever was to become my fate. As I looked around, I realized something that informs the way I live to this day: It was at that moment I realized the difference between options and choices.

Options Are What Life Gives Us. Choice Is What We Do with Them.

And so I made my choice. I picked option number three and I decided I had an opportunity. I had nothing to draw from besides my memory, and the feeling of peace that was settling over me, but that was enough to move me into the alchemy of life's greatest transformation.

As I've mentioned, a little over one year before the kidnapping, my mother died. She was just barely fifty-seven, and we lost her suddenly; it was an epic tragedy. I was still very much dealing with my grief when everything happened, and I had been considering taking a sabbatical from work to go and just sit in an ashram somewhere and grieve it all out. I was young and naive and thought I could go and just get it all out and done with. The morning of my "great realization," I discovered that maybe I had gotten what I wanted. I looked around me and realized I had an interesting opportunity in front of me. I also discerned that I had three things I would probably never have again (if I made it out of this thing in one piece!): I had time, God only knew how much time I had, I had solitude—the desert can be a very peaceful place when you aren't being terrorized by your kidnappers, and I had nothing to do. I surveyed my surroundings and decided that maybe this was my ashram. While I didn't exactly have the emotional freedom to grieve the loss of my mother, I realized quite quickly that I had complete control over what was happening in my mind. Yes, my body was being held hostage, but they couldn't get into my head, no matter how hard they tried—that was all mine.

So, I decided to get really organized in my mind, and I made a work plan for myself. I figured I had the time, so why not face some things in my life, some decisions, behaviors, beliefs, reactions, and evaluate them, examine them, and then . . . perhaps, let them go. I started at my very first memory, when my mother took me to the movie theater when I was four. We went to see *Snow White and the Seven Dwarfs*, and I could still see her, dressed in a blue sun dress with little white flowers covering the fabric. I could remember how suntanned her arms were, and all the freckles that ran up and down her arms, giving clues that we spent our summer days at the city pool. I didn't know the difference between fantasy and reality and so I made her wait until the entire movie theater emptied out because I was so sure Snow White and all her dwarves were going to come out and greet me in the end. I remembered the shape of my mom's teeth when she laughed when she realized what I was waiting for—and as

I sat there, at the base of that tree, mind traveling over two decades into the past, I found a place of peace and safety I hadn't even been able to access outside of captivity.

I went through every single date my husband Erik and I had been on. I relived our conversations in my mind. The ones where, just a few weeks in, we both knew what we were feeling was for real, and I committed myself to our relationship, once again. I had no idea if I was ever going to see him again, but I had faith and peace in knowing that I had done the right thing by marrying him, and I felt confident that he was doing everything in his power to get me out of there.

One by one, the memories played out before me like the scenes in another movie that I was watching. This practice not only kept me sane and tethered to reality, but it gave me a place where I alone was in charge.

I was sequestered to an eight-by-six-foot mat under an acacia tree, being held hostage by dozens of heavily armed Somali pirates—but the interesting thing I realized throughout the course of my captivity was, my body was being detained, but in my mind, I had never been freer. There, in that captivity, I was somehow able to create order from chaos. I built a sacred space in my mind as I faced the hardest parts of myself, examined my grief, my fear, my regrets. I reflected on the loss of my mother and the ache of unfinished grief that came with losing her. And slowly, I came to understand that while my captors had taken my freedom, they hadn't taken *me*.

Surviving Survival Is a Sacred Choice

As I sat beneath that acacia tree, I realized something I've carried with me ever since: Surviving survival is not something that just *happens* to us—it's something we have to *choose*. The options may be handed to us by circumstance, but the choice is ours to make. And in that moment, mine became clear.

I chose to turn captivity into contemplation.

I chose to mine meaning from grief.

I chose to transform waiting into work.

I chose to reclaim the only freedom I had—my mind—and begin the long, internal journey of healing from the inside out.

Those choices didn't change my circumstances, but they changed *me*. And that made all the difference.

Every survivor will one day face the same invitation: to stay tethered to what happened or to begin weaving something new from the threads of their pain. One path keeps you locked in the identity of victimhood. The other, while harder, unlocks the possibility of becoming someone wiser, deeper, and more alive than you were before.

You may not have chosen what hurt you. But you *can* choose what you do with it.

Surviving survival means making meaning where others see only loss. It means building something beautiful in the ruins and choosing your voice over your silence, your agency over your helplessness.

Your future over your past.

This is your ashram. This is your tree. This is your moment to decide: Will I survive this and stay stuck in the story, or will I choose to shape what comes next?

The choice is yours. And that is your power.

* * *

There are many challenges in learning how to mine meaning from what you have endured and turn it into something that not only serves your healing but also contributes to the world.

Meaning-making does not happen passively; it is an active process. You must choose to engage with your experience, extract the lessons, and shape your story into a tool for growth. This chapter will guide you through that process, helping you reclaim your voice and use it as a force for good.

Survivor Spotlight: Caitlin Myers—Choosing Resilience After the Wreckage

Caitlin Myers never imagined that a relationship formed in college would lead her to the brink of death. Her boyfriend Dave was not just controlling—he was a bully, a volatile presence who chipped away at her confidence until she barely recognized herself. But the defining moment of their toxic relationship came in a flash of twisted metal and broken glass.

Dave picked her up from the airport one evening, and in a seemingly reckless act of rage and immaturity, he drove at dangerous speeds—ultimately losing control of the car. Caitlin was launched from the vehicle at nearly 90 miles per hour, her body slamming onto a busy highway. A stranger—an everyday passerby—risked their own life to shield her from oncoming traffic. She flatlined en route to the hospital. It would be months before she could sit upright, let alone stand. Dave walked away from the accident with barely a scratch.

Her injuries were catastrophic: a shattered pelvis, facial fractures, a paralyzed leg, and a wired-shut jaw. Caitlin endured excruciating chronic pain and agonizing withdrawals from the painkillers she had become dependent on—fentanyl, specifically. In her book *Shattered: From Wreckage to Resilience*, she recounts the withdrawal pain being so awful that she actually ripped her own hair out. The easy choice would have been for Cait to surrender to despair and live the rest of her life in pain and addiction—no one would have blamed her. But Caitlin made a different choice and she decided to survive survival.

She chose to believe healing was possible, even when doctors said otherwise. She chose to detox from the opioids and rebuild her strength with nourishing foods and mindful habits, even when people were skeptical. She chose to take back her power by holding her abuser accountable by taking him to court. And, eventually, when she was ready, she chose to help others—transforming her pain into purpose by becoming a wellness coach for those navigating chronic pain and physical recovery.

Caitlin chronicles the long road back to herself in her memoir making the important point that her story is not just about surviving a near-fatal crash. It's about reclaiming her agency after abuse, about choosing truth and transformation over numbness and despair. It's a story of power, forged in pain, and a fierce reminder that healing is not passive. It's a choice made—sometimes over and over again—against all odds.

How Caitlin's Story Reflects the RISE Framework
R – Reckon with the Pain

Caitlin faced the raw truth of both physical devastation and emotional abuse. She did not deny the wreckage—of her body or her relationship. Reckoning, for her, meant acknowledging the full scope of what was lost and broken.

I – Identify the Impact

She traced the long-term consequences of trauma: addiction, depression, chronic pain, and shattered self-trust. But she also became aware of the lies she had internalized about her worth and her ability to heal.

S – Seek the Meaning

In the quiet aftermath, Caitlin began to ask: *What if this pain could teach me something?* She saw how her healing could serve others. She found meaning in advocacy, in rebuilding her life through wellness, and in writing her story.

E – Embody the Purpose

Now, Caitlin lives out her purpose as a wellness coach, author, and advocate. She doesn't just speak about resilience—she embodies it, guiding others who are navigating the long, painful road back to themselves.

PAUSE, PONDER, AND PROCESS

What options were placed in front of you after your trauma—and what choice did you make?

1. Where in your story do you still feel like the pain is choosing *you*—and how might you begin to take that power back?

2. What deeper invitation might your pain be offering you right now?

3. What meaning is quietly waiting for you to uncover it beneath the noise?

4. Where might you be surviving by default—and what would it look like to move into intentional living?

5. What truth wants to surface if you stop resisting and start listening to your experience?

6. **Which values have become clearer or more important because of what you've been through?**

7. **If you believed this moment had spiritual purpose, how would you show up differently?**

RISE Reminders

- I didn't choose what happened to me—but I *can* choose what comes next.
- Life gives me options. I decide what becomes my choice.
- Surviving is something that happened to me. Surviving survival is something I do for myself.
- Even when everything feels out of my control, my mind is still mine to lead.
- Meaning doesn't arrive all at once. But it's always there, waiting for me to begin asking the right questions.
- I am not stuck—I am standing at a crossroads. The next move is mine to choose.

CHAPTER 9
WE DON'T RISE ALONE

Being a former hostage is lonely. Being a former female hostage compounds that loneliness tenfold. In all my years after captivity, I have only met with a handful of people who have experienced something even remotely similar to me, and while it is always refreshing to have conversations with someone who can identify with the trauma I have endured, those talks have been few and far between.

That said, I have been incredibly fortunate to have a family, a husband, and a group of close friends who have stuck by me and supported me throughout my whole life, especially in these darkest moments. When I consider what enables some people to be more resilient than others, I often think about the things that we can't control: personalities, character traits, support networks, as well as tools that have been acquired throughout our lives—and some of us have had the opportunity and stability to acquire more than others, certainly, but one defining factor between those who can reframe their most challenging moments and turn them into contribution, has to be the gift of community.

One of the unfortunate outcomes for many hostages in the aftermath of their release is the dismantling of family and support systems. The time after release can be tough for the former hostage and their family, depending on so many things, such as the length of time the hostage was held, whether there was a ransom demand that needed to be paid, and who was handling the negotiations and the payments for ransom, if that is the situation. Many families are divided by the trauma that an event like this will cause as they are thrust into financial ruin or the media spotlight due to no fault of their own. Many are not in financial positions to pay out millions for ransom demands and are forced to liquidate assets, sell houses, and drain their retirement funds to come up with the money needed to "maybe" see their loved ones back home in one piece.

My heart breaks for the hostage who returns and has no family or support network to catch them and help ease them back into normal daily life—which is why the work of Hostage US is so important. My heart breaks for anyone who has experienced significant trauma and has felt like they have to manage their surviving survival alone. My experience has led me to believe that those who are able to put their lives back together in the aftermath of trauma largely are able to do so because of the support and community they have around them, willing to pick them up, day in and day out, and remind them they are loved and valued.

According to the World Health Organization,[5] people who have a strong social network are less likely to develop symptoms associated with post-traumatic stress disorder when having experienced trauma. Having a network of people around us, who love us and are willing to hold space for us, pick up the phone and talk us

---

5   "Post-traumatic Stress Disorder," World Health Organization, published May 27, 2024, https://www.who.int/news-room/fact-sheets/detail/post-traumatic-stress-disorder.

through the terror when we are having a flashback, or take a walk with us when we are feeling at our most alone . . . goes a long way for the one who is healing. It is critical for our healing outcome to have freedom to express our emotions, our regrets, and our newfound revelations with those who know us and have committed to seeing us through the hard days.

According to a study conducted at Berkeley,[6] our ability to be resilient and to believe we are worthy of survival, and then what comes after, often has more to do with our social support than it does with our individual strengths.

Dr. Elliott Friedman, a resilience researcher and professor of human development from Purdue University, found through his research that "the availability of social support in all its forms— instrumental support, emotional support, support with how you think about things—they all matter and help us in facing challenges."[7]

So much of our research and what we know about resilience is based on individual experiences, and when digging into the steps I used to build my toolkit, I knew that an important part of my healing experience was directly correlated to the strong support I felt, in particular, from my family. I know how lucky I am, and I am truly grateful for all the love they have shown me, both while I was in captivity and after.

Despite my closeness with my family and their unwavering support, as the dust settled and they oriented themselves enough to pick up their lives where they had left them on October 25, 2011, I found myself feeling very isolated and alone. My recollection of

---

6   Jill Suttie, "Four Ways Social Support Makes You More Resilient," *Great Good Magazine*, November 13, 2017, https://greatergood.berkeley.edu/article/item/ four_ways_social_support_makes_you_more_resilient.

7   Friedman, Elliot et al. "Social Connectedness, Functional Capacity, and Longevity: A Focus on Positive Relations with Others," *Social Science & Medicine* 340 (2024): 116419. doi:10.1016/j.socscimed.2023.116419.

those times in my life is filled with pain and sadness, and I hate thinking about how incredibly alone and bewildered I felt. Still, I need to go back to that place to unpack how important building community is for our healing and how worthwhile the massive effort and emotional risk it truly is when rebuilding a life after survival.

* * *

In the aftermath of the success of *Impossible Odds*, my husband Erik and I were presented with many opportunities to share our story with a variety of audiences. As a teacher, I found this to be incredibly exciting because I got to drop back into my role as a storyteller; I found that, essentially, I was still getting to teach a lesson. It wasn't fourth-grade math anymore, but rather key takeaways I had learned from spending all that time alone in the desert. The lessons and message have evolved since I started speaking, but getting to share my story of *Impossible Odds* is still one of my favorite things about what I get to do now. It was directly after one of these talks that we met a man named Jim LeBlanc. This particular audience was comprised of security professionals and Jim was there because he had spent time working as a chief of staff running an NGO in Iraq. He immediately connected with our story, given his own security run-ins, and approached us after the keynote was finished. We struck up a conversation that quickly evolved into a friendship.

Over the years, Jim became a trusted mentor and advisor to both of us, but to me, in particular. As I was swirling in trauma and indecision, trying desperately to figure out what my next steps were, I would periodically reach out to Jim for advice, and he allowed me to use him as a sounding board for ideas that were brewing in exchange for lunch! I often felt completely out of my professional depth when talking with Jim, but he was always kind, compassionate, and nonjudgmental. He was generous with his introductions, and it was through him that I connected with a newly established nonprofit based in Washington, DC, called Hostage US.

Through my association with Hostage US, I came into contact with many people who were committed to the cause of bringing American hostages and wrongfully detained individuals home. I met with families who were going through similar struggles as my family had due to their loved ones being wrongfully detained or held hostage in different parts of the world. There was a sense of community that I had not experienced since I had been rescued, and while we were a small group of individuals, we were connected because of our painfully unfortunate circumstances. Still, the commitment to advocate, educate, and produce results that would include bringing people home from terrible conditions was significant to me.

In addition to Hostage US, Jim introduced me to other strong women in his professional circle, two of which became great mentors to me, and it was through one of them that I met Krista Clive-Smith, the founder of Merack Publishing, through which Soul Speak Press, my publishing imprint, was born. My friendship with these women grew over several years and multiple conversations in which I had to allow myself to be professionally vulnerable and just ask questions. I didn't know what I was doing, I didn't know what I wanted to do, and I didn't know what I was qualified to do for work anymore. I was overwhelmed and scared much of the time. Afraid of inconveniencing people or that I was asking for too much when I met with them for dinner; I had to pull up my big girl panties and just *ask*. Fortunately, everyone I met with was kind to me, and I will forever be grateful to every single person who met with me for dinner, listened to me patiently, and gave me honest feedback.

One dinner with my friend Monica stands out. Monica is tall, a gorgeous redhead who had made millions in the finance industry, spent most of her career living and working in London and roaming around other glamorous locations in Europe; an added plus was that she was super funny! I loved the way she told stories with well-manicured hands that were always moving when she described her latest dating disaster or told me about a professional endeavor that she had just achieved. We were sharing a plate of hummus at a tiny Greek restaurant in the touristy part of Alexandria, Virginia, one evening when it was my turn to update her on my life. I had been feeling incredibly frustrated at the time, my wheels spinning as I tried to figure out what I was supposed to be doing with my life. I was in a good place, emotionally and mentally, and ready to create something or join a purpose-driven cause, but I just couldn't figure out what mattered to me. Everything that had mattered, in regard to work and my overall worldview had been left in Africa. I was exhausted most of the time because I was so focused on "figuring it out" which was obvious when I told her that I kept having this recurring dream. For several nights I would wake up dreaming that I was trapped beneath a wall of ice. I would be working desperately to pickax my way through this wall because I knew that it was keeping me separated from my purpose on the other side. I was tired, but I didn't feel frantic or panicked in the dream. I just knew what awaited me on the other side of the ice was what was "next," and I was so ready for it, I just couldn't stand it.

I remember Monica listening intently to my recount, asking her what she thought it all meant. She was silent for a few moments, then took a sip of her white wine and looked me directly in the eye, and said, "But Jess, there is *no* ice. You can do or be whatever you want—and no one can stop you."

It was one of those moments that hung in the air, just long enough for me to catch up to what she knew, the moment I opened my mouth. The ice was a metaphor for my own self-imposed limitations in this dream. My subconscious was trying to tell me that I was banging my head against these barriers that only existed because I put them there. I was in control of taking them down—or if we stick with the ice analogy, breaking through to the other side. What I hadn't told her was that at the end of the dream, I would collapse in exhaustion and lay down only to discover there was a tunnel that had already been hollowed out. I hadn't seen it because I was so busy trying to bust my way through the thick ice.

Truth be told, I was still very stuck in the "yesterday" even though I claimed to be in hot pursuit of the "tomorrow." I had one foot in Africa and one foot in the US because I was petrified that if I let go of my work there and my love for the life there and the people and everything I had experienced, I would never be able to go back. I had this subconscious belief that if I actually let go of my yearning to be who I used to be in the place I used to be it, that it would be lost to me forever. Almost as if it had never existed in the first place. And if all of that, my life, my longing, my pursuit of purpose had never existed . . . had I?

It was clear that resistance was manifesting, even in my dreams. Why it was illustrated as an ice cave, I don't know, but I do understand the significance now.

Oh, how I fought this new life of mine! All that trying and energy wasted, hanging on to the past, sinking back down into my grief because it was safe and familiar, and well, it was my right to feel bad, wasn't it? It was then that I realized it was all my efforts that were largely futile, to hold on to the past that were leaving me too exhausted to actually feel my way into the future—my next phase of purpose. It wasn't until I started to relinquish my tight grip on the past that I then began to make room for what would become in my future. It took me way too long, in my opinion, to learn that holding on to what *was* is the surest way to crowd out the space we need for creativity and enlightenment that will move us into our destiny. While Monica claimed there was no wall, I realized she was right, at least on the fact that it had not been superimposed by anyone else. The wall, in fact, was me.

That conversation with Monica was quite literally life-changing that night, and I'm forever grateful to her for her time and insight. I walked out of that interaction with her feeling so free. There was, indeed, no wall of ice, if I just got myself out of the way and stopped trying so hard, I could do anything I wanted to do.

The point of being in community is multifaceted. Yes, we need support. Yes, we need understanding. But sometimes, what we really need is a kick in the ass in the form of the truth. And sometimes, those closest to us can be saying the same things, over and over again, but we can't hear it until it comes from someone else, who is not so invested in our reality.

Monica was that for me. I doubt she even remembers the conversation, but that is how it is with community. When you are networked with individuals who move in such a way as to light the whole world up, they just trust that the way they function and show up is enough. And with her, it was more than.

* * *

About the same time I was having these conversations with Monica and Jim, and engaging with Krista about branding and exploring the world of publishing, I began writing quite a bit. I had been diving deep into my thoughts and feelings around survival and how to build resilience, as well as the grief that comes in waves in the aftermath of trauma in a personal blog called *The Survivor's Well*. Week after week, I moved deeper into my writing to process my trauma, and also, really, to connect with others who might have some insight and could offer emotional support in a time when I so badly needed it. The responses were mostly positive, although I would imagine there were posts that some felt were a bit of an overshare at times. Still, again, when you are bleeding out emotionally, you are desperate for someone to find you and hold your hand and just say, "Hey, I see you. You are not alone."

One of the people who did that for me was a woman named Kathy Callahan. She was a writer in her own right, and she and her husband had become friends of ours as soon as we moved to the US. We met her husband Tom at the gym one afternoon when Erik was waiting for me to finish a yoga class and was holding our eight-month-old August, trying to keep him occupied until I was done. Tom came out of the weight room and made eye contact with our gorgeous boy, and the two connected—both old souls, it takes one to know one. So drawn in by my baby boy's deep, dark brown eyes, Tom couldn't help but come over and introduce himself. It turned out that we had much in common with Tom and Kathy, as they had spent some time living in South Africa and Tom was experienced in the international development world, as was Erik. We hit it off, and over time, they became a treasured part of our community.

It was Kathy who reached out to me and said, "Hey, I have someone I want you to meet!" This was after I had asked to join her writing group, which was well-established. She took my request to them, and they said no, much to my astonishment! Another friend of Kathy's had done the same thing, and she, too, had been rejected. I guess when you get the right group together, no one is willing to mess with the dynamics. While I was a bit miffed about being rejected, (I mean, I have a *NYT* bestseller for God's sake!) I did understand. Kathy told me she had another fellow writer friend who was also named Jessica and was posting beautifully written posts on Facebook intermittently. She thought she should do something more serious about her writing and so proposed a "blind writing date" dinner so she could introduce the two of us.

Over an enormous plate of fried cauliflower, Jess and I dove deep immediately, and I felt this sense of being seen and understood, in a way I had been craving, but hadn't known how to articulate until it happened. I could tell by the look on Kathy's face that she was extremely proud of her authors' meet-cute! Jess and I exchanged information and planned to discuss establishing our own writing group. We followed through and brought in a few other women who were all working on various writing projects. About a month later, the time came for us to meet and exchange feedback, and Jess and I found ourselves back at a table again, just the two of us this time— minus the enormous plate of cauliflower! No one else had bothered to show up, so we carried on with feedback for each other's work. As we shared with each other what we loved about the writing, as well as what we still had questions about, I offhandedly mentioned that I had been thinking about starting a podcast. I was obsessed with my pursuit of having real, authentic conversations; I sensed that vulnerability and talking about the "real stuff" was just as important to her, but she caught me off guard when she immediately connected with the idea, and within weeks, our podcast became a reality when our show, "We Should Talk About That" (WeSTAT), was born.

We couldn't have known when we launched in January 2020 that in just a few months, we would be stuck at home, figuring out how to record virtually instead of in studio like we had been doing, or that because everyone in the world was quarantining and bored, we would have the opportunity to interview a much higher caliber of guests than we would have been able to if we had been in studio. Before we knew it, we had reached the top 1 percent of all podcasts being downloaded worldwide! When sheltering-in-place requirements lifted, we began hosting live recordings in our city of Alexandria, Virginia, and we built a community of women (and a few loyal men!) one authentic conversation at a time. For three years, we worked tirelessly to research, hold space for these conversations, and interview exciting guests, like Melodie Beatty, the mother of trauma therapy, Candace Bushnell, the creator of *Sex in the City*, and Eve Rodsky, the author of *Fair Play*, which inspired the *FAIR PLAY* documentary from Reese Witherspoon's production company Hello Sunshine. Not only were we working toward a purpose that felt meaningful and relevant, especially at a time in history when things were so complicated and there were many issues to discuss, but we were also able to lean on each other, collaborate on something we really believed in, and turn our time into what we believed was a meaningful contribution to the world. This project, this purpose, and the community that came along because of it, helped me heal tremendously by giving me so much in the way of direction, goals to achieve, and just plain fun!

The first two episodes we recorded stand out to me the most. They were just conversations between Jess and I, but they were incredibly important conversations for me, especially. The first one was establishing our mission for the show—the fact that we were going to all this trouble and effort to host conversations so that others would feel less isolated and alone, felt very aligned and right for me at that moment. The second conversation we had was all about my kidnapping. While I had been talking about my experience in a variety of capacities for years, this felt different. I opened myself up to become more vulnerable, as our WeSTAT audience was mostly comprised of my neighbors and people who perhaps knew of me from preschool drop-off or soccer games but didn't know the extent of what I had been through. It felt as if I was coming out of the kidnapping closet and I felt so incredibly light and free afterward.

I had spent years wrongfully believing that if people knew the truth of what I had been through, they would think I was a freak. In my mind, no one could possibly endure something so strangely traumatic as being held hostage in the desert for ninety-three days and then come out on the other side of such a trauma as a normal person. It's interesting to me now that I spent so much time and energy wrongly judging other people, and myself through other people's eyes. I would imagine I am not alone in that practice, and I believe it is the false narratives we are telling ourselves, about what we have done, or what we have been through that keeps us from making meaningfully healthy connections.

One might wonder why anyone would even need to know what has happened to us. Why couldn't I just keep that part of myself, and my story, tucked away? Why did it have to be at the forefront of every interaction I had? I tried, believe me. It's not like I walked up to people, held out my hand, and said, "Hi, I'm Jess. And I was kidnapped in Somalia." The challenge of not speaking about my kidnapping was due to the high-profile media exposure it had, combined with the relocating and starting over of life, that no matter how hard I tried to avoid it, the topic inevitably came up. People would look at me as if I had sprouted another head when I told them what had happened and who I was. Or at least, I believed that is what they were seeing. Most likely it was a mixture of reality and projection. Because I felt ashamed and self-conscious and weird, it was hard to open up. I would largely keep to myself on the playground when I pushed my son on the swings, or when I was attending a meet-up group for writers. Ironically, the more I talked about "it" though, the more open about my experience I became, and the more I embraced my story and all I had been through; it was extremely empowering! I experienced this empowerment one afternoon, after Erik and I were at the toddler park, and he was actually the one to answer a host of questions from a mom who was there to let her twins run around. I stood on the perimeter of the sandbox, straining my ear to hear how much he was saying to her. When he was done with the story, she came over to me, introduced herself, and invited me to come speak at her book club. It's been almost eleven years since we met her on the playground, and she and I are still very close friends. It took me a while to realize, but I was the one who was looking at myself as if I had sprouted an extra head. It took me much therapy to get to a place where I didn't care how people reacted anymore, because I felt strong and proud of my resilience.

The most challenging part of building community is being honest and vulnerable about what you have been through—especially when you decide you want to make your mark and turn your pain into something purposeful to help others. We can fall into the trap of believing that we need to be 100 percent healed and have it all together before we can make an impact, certainly, or even before we can make connections. This is not true and it will keep us from doing important work to further our own healing experience, as well as from helping others who are waiting to hear what we have been through in order to not feel so isolated and alone. I use a saying with my writing students and authors when I am teaching memoir writing workshops that applies perfectly in this situation: "First get it out, then get it right." We often use this for first drafts of manuscripts, but it parallels nicely to anything we are going to try. Yes, we must take into account impact as it relates to intention. Still, so many people stay stuck in their muck because they are paralyzed by perfection, or scared of being seen for who they truly are, resulting in missed opportunities for further healing for us and those in our surrounding community.

Over the years, I have committed myself to being open to the opportunity to connect, no matter where I find myself. Whether I am at a speaking event for a few hours or I am working with a cohort of twenty women for the better part of a year for one of our writing projects, or even if I'm being driven home from the airport by a Lyft driver; I have made a commitment to myself, and those around me: I am available for connection. It's this availability that others have given to me, that has helped clear the path I have walked to wholeness in my life, and indeed, this is a gift I want to pay forward.

Trauma can make us sensitive to closeness, rendering us afraid to connect with others. Pain can make us skittish of trusting because we have been hurt before and our primitive instincts just want to protect us from that danger again. Whatever you have been through may have taken everything you had to survive, first the ordeal, and then later, the outcome. But connecting with others—especially those who may have experienced something like us—or allowing ourselves to open up to someone who might be willing and able to help us, not only provides the support we so badly need to heal and rehabilitate, but it validates our human experience as well as provides us with a sense of belonging.

One of the most heart wrenching impacts of my kidnapping experience was the fact that it made me feel freakishly misunderstood. I remember meeting a new mom friend when my son was about eight months old—I was so excited to connect with her as our children crawled around the playroom of the rec center after storytime. I was doing my best to maintain general answers about who I was and where I had come from. On our third playdate, she had put it together and figured out who I was. I remember blurting out, "I'm not crazy!" to her when she asked me if I was the same Jessica Buchanan who had been kidnapped and rescued by SEAL Team Six just a year earlier. It was so awkward, and I had to work very hard to keep myself from bursting into tears. I felt so exposed and embarrassed about everything, and wondered how it was going to affect my children making friends in the future. We didn't really see much of each other after that, and I was disappointed—both in her, and myself. I've learned, over the years, how to share about my trauma in a way that makes people feel like they don't have to take care of me, which also helps me feel safe. When we can establish a community that feels accepting of our story and supportive of our healing journey, we will all benefit in many ways.

There were many dark days in my trauma healing where I felt shame and regret and engaged in self-blame. I would cycle through anger at my organization for sending me to such a dangerous place where something like this could happen or break out into a cold sweat when I thought about all the things that could have gone wrong during my rescue operation, including loss of life to one or many of SEAL Team Six. Cognitively, I knew I had not been included in the decision-making when it came to issuing the order for my rescue, but I had ended up in this terrible situation because I had not stood up for myself. When I started talking more openly, especially with other women, about this idea of abandoning myself and letting my voice be stifled, it made me feel validated in a way that is hard to quantify. While my circumstances were wildly different from many others, the driving forces that got me into that situation were universal. In talking and writing in community, I was able to create my second publication, *Deserts to Mountaintops: Our Collective Journey to (re)Claiming Our Voice*, and it was a huge success because the stories, written by twenty-four women, made others, both in the group of writers, and the readers and beyond, feel connected, validated, and understood. Feeling seen is essential to building community, but feeling understood by that community is what helps further our healing because we know we are safe enough to tell our stories, the real, true parts of what has happened to us, and what we have learned as we have struggled to survive.

When our trust has been violated, our goodness taken advantage of, it is understandably difficult to picture ourselves forming meaningful connections because our past traumas make us feel unsafe. But the restoration and reprieve that we can feel when we find ourselves in communion with good people who are emitting positive energy into our world not only helps ease the fear and exhaustion of learning to trust again, but it also allows our nervous system to relax and begin to regulate. The more experience we allow ourselves to have in the safety of true connection, the better we are going to get at co-regulating our emotions. I know it is scary to think about being in the company of someone you are not sure your emotions, your story, and especially your reactions are safe with. When you can settle into relationships or have social interactions that are positive and affirming, your body releases oxytocin, the hormone that produces feelings of trust and emotional connection. I think of these interactions as a balm to my hurting heart—just like an antibiotic ointment keeps out germs and reduces our chances of infection and the pain worsening, so too is the impact of a positive social connection with a safe and heart-centered friend.

Community is essential for us to move forward with our lives. It gives us purpose, as we strive for direction and clarity to our life's calling, as well as provides a sense of belonging, and inspiration for what can become of our pain as we are empowered to take action and not surrender to just becoming a bystander in our survival journey. Is it possible to build resilience without community, connection, and support? Sure, anything is possible. But it will be harder, take longer, and be a lot less fun! The whole point of building a support system and finding a place where we feel like we belong is so that when the hard times come, we have that social safety net that will catch us when we feel like we are in freefall.

Hubert Humphrey, the thirty-eighth vice president of the United States said it simply, and said it best: "The greatest healing therapy is friendship and love."

I couldn't agree more.

Meyli Chapin—Surviving Alone, Then Building Community

On January 15, 2019, Meyli Chapin's life changed in a single day. While on a business trip in Nairobi, Kenya, for her employer Google, she became trapped inside the DusitD2 hotel complex as the terrorist group al-Shabaab launched a deadly coordinated attack. For hours, she hid silently in a room while suicide bombers and gunmen swept the building. Twenty-one people died that day. Meyli survived—but her survival marked the beginning of a very different kind of struggle.

What followed was not just trauma, but disconnection. PTSD made her feel untethered from the world she once moved through with ease. She couldn't relate to anyone—she didn't fit in with her family, her friends, not even in her own mind. In a moment of desperation, Meyli googled "support groups for victims of terrorist attacks" and came up with nothing. That absence of understanding and support was deafening. She began to wonder: *Am I the only one who feels this way? Will I be stuck like this forever? Will I ever feel joy again?*

Working with a therapist was a turning point that Meyli says saved her life. She remembers one day in particular, when her therapist went through a routine list of symptoms related to PTSD and asked if she was experiencing any of them—and when Meyli said yes to every one, her therapist simply nodded and replied, "That's all very normal."

Meyli burst into tears. No one had told her that before. Suddenly, she didn't feel so unmoored.

That moment of realization lit the spark for a meaningful mission: If so many people were hurting the way she was, but couldn't access a therapist to hear those words, what would happen to them? What were they supposed to cling to? Knowing that trauma skews to those who are socioeconomically challenged and who have very little access to mental health support, Meyli felt overwhelmed by the reality that so many people were hurting and could never get better based on lack of privilege.

Meyli couldn't stand by and know so many people were experiencing similar debilitating symptoms, so she built something.

With her Stanford education, experience working at Google, and a heart burning with purpose, Meyli and her husband created Trauma Brace—a twelve-week, app-based therapeutic program grounded in evidence-based PTSD treatment. Designed for survivors of all kinds of trauma, Trauma Brace delivers the gold standard of therapy in an accessible, private, and structured format. Users receive personalized progress tracking, symptom assessments, and guided healing assignments. The app is HIPAA compliant, scientifically informed, and culturally responsive—it's even been translated into Ukrainian and distributed to survivors of war, free of charge.

What started as a response to terrorist violence has since become a lifeline for thousands—especially young women recovering from sexual assault. Many of them say they never would have sought in-person help, but the anonymity of the app gave them a safe starting point. Some use it to bridge the gap to therapy. Others find real relief within its structure.

Meyli remembers something her FBI victim specialist told her in the early days of her healing: She said, "I know you don't want to hear this right now, because no one wants to hear about silver linings, but believe me, you may feel all alone right now, but someday, you'll look into the eyes of another survivor, and you'll understand each other on a level no one else can." *That is community*.

Meyli didn't find that community when she needed it.

So she created it—for all of us.

How Meyli's Story Reflects the RISE Framework
R – Reckon with the Pain

Meyli had to face not just the trauma of surviving a terrorist attack, but the isolation that followed. The lack of support systems for victims of terrorism left her feeling like she didn't belong anywhere anymore. Her grief wasn't just about what happened in Nairobi—it was about what happened afterward: the silence, the disconnection, and the loss of joy.

I – Identify the Impact

The PTSD symptoms Meyli experienced began to define her every-day life—flashbacks, panic, emotional numbness, and a deep sense of otherness. She felt unrecognizable in her former world. She realized that her trauma wasn't just an emotional event—it was reshaping her identity, relationships, and sense of safety.

S – Seek the Meaning

When a therapist told her that everything she was experiencing was normal, something clicked. If others felt like this too, why weren't there more tools to help? Meyli began asking not just how she could heal, but how she could ensure that others wouldn't have to feel as alone as she did. She began looking for ways to turn her pain into purpose.

E – Embody the Purpose

Meyli built Trauma Brace, an evidence-based app designed to give trauma survivors access to therapeutic tools when therapy itself is out of reach. She partnered with universities, translated the program for war survivors, and became an advocate for those living in the long shadow of trauma. Her recovery became a blueprint for others—and her mission became building the community she once searched for and never found.

Steps to Building Community

While resilience can be built alone, connection often makes the process more effective. Even if you don't have close community support now, seeking books, online resources, or personal practices can help build inner strength until you're ready or able to connect with others.

Building community after trauma can feel overwhelming, especially if trust has been broken or isolation has become a habit. However, reconnecting with others is a crucial step in healing. Here's a step-by-step suggestion to help you build meaningful connections in a way that feels safe and empowering:

1. **Start with yourself: Rebuild inner safety**
   Before seeking community, begin by nurturing self-trust and emotional safety.
   - **Acknowledge your needs:** What kind of support do you crave? Encouragement, companionship, or deep understanding?
   - **Practice self-compassion:** Trauma can make us feel unworthy of connection. Remind yourself that you deserve community. Did you know self-compassion is a core component of building resilience? And that struggling is a sign that things are moving in the right direction? When there is discomfort, that means there is often growth.
     » How do you practice self-compassion in your life?
     » How can you be more compassionate to yourself if you are not?
     » When is a time you have demonstrated self-compassion?
   - **Set boundaries:** Knowing your limits will help you engage with others without feeling overwhelmed. What kind of boundaries can you put in place as you begin to branch out and build connections?
   - **Practice self-reliance while remaining open to connection**

> » Learn to trust yourself and your ability to navigate hard times. While you can build resilience alone, remain open to future connections that may support your journey.

2. **Take small, safe steps toward connection**

   Rebuilding relationships doesn't have to be all at once. Start small:

   - **Reconnect with trusted individuals:** Reach out to a supportive friend or family member, even if it's just a short message.
   - **Join safe, low-pressure spaces:** Attend events where interaction is optional, like a book club, a hobby group, or a yoga class.
   - **Engage in online communities:** If in-person feels too much, online support groups related to healing, shared interests, or mental wellness can be a great first step.

3. **Seek trauma-informed spaces**

   Surrounding yourself with people who understand trauma and healing makes connection easier. I'm not suggesting you form trauma bonds, but I do know that you will feel more seen and understood when you engage with others who have been through something, know something, and want to teach you something.

   - **Therapy groups or support circles:** Whether through a therapist, religious group, or local organizations, support groups create a safe space to share and listen. Have you honestly given this a try? If not, why not? Make a list of groups in your area that you could possibly attend, and then give it a try!

- **Creative or movement-based communities:** Art, music, and activities like dance or martial arts help process emotions while connecting with like-minded individuals. Perhaps your skills, talents, and interests in this way of healing will also lead you to your purpose. What have you not engaged in for a long while, and could try again?
- **Spiritual or mindfulness groups:** Meditation circles, faith-based communities, or retreats can offer grounding support. Are you open to finding connection through spirituality? Why or why not?

4. **Build reciprocity: Give & receive support**
   - **Practice active listening:** Healing happens when we feel heard, but also when we hold space for others.
   - **Volunteer or help others:** Contributing to a cause can create meaningful connections while fostering purpose. What causes do you care about? If you don't know, it's time to explore!
   - **Be open to vulnerability in small steps:** You don't have to share your entire story at once, but allowing others to see parts of your authentic self fosters trust. How can you start sharing small parts of your authentic self? Who can you start sharing them with?

5. **Be patient with the process**
   - Healing and connection take time—allow yourself to go at your own pace. Remember, it takes the time it needs to take. No more, no less. What surprises you about the timeline of your healing and connection journey?
   - Not every interaction will lead to deep connection, and that's okay. Focus on quality over quantity.

- If a situation or person doesn't feel safe, honor your instincts and step back without guilt.

6. **Stay open to new possibilities**
   - The right community may not always look like what you expected. Stay open to different types of connections.
   - Be curious about people's experiences—sometimes, healing happens in unexpected relationships.
   - Trust that even if you've been hurt before, there are kind, understanding people out there.

Healing in community doesn't mean relying on others to fix us—it means allowing relationships to help us grow, witness our journey, and remind us that we're not alone. You are worthy of connection, and step by step, you can create a community that nurtures your healing.

PAUSE, PONDER, AND PROCESS

1. **What has been your experience with community during or after your trauma?**
   Have you felt supported, isolated, or somewhere in between?

2. **Who has been part of your healing journey—and how have they impacted you?**
   Are there people you haven't yet acknowledged for the role they played?

3. **What internal "walls of ice" might still be keeping you from fully connecting with others?**
    What fears, beliefs, or past experiences are influencing your openness?

4. **Have you ever believed, even subconsciously, that your story made you "too much" for others?**
    What would it take to challenge that belief?

5. **Where in your life are you resisting connection—and what might happen if you softened that resistance?**

6. **What would it look like for you to be available for connection in your current season of life?**
    What's one small way you can make yourself more open to meaningful relationships?

7. **What kind of community do you most crave—and what steps can you take to start building or finding it?**

8. **When have you felt truly *seen* and *understood* by someone else?**
    How did that moment shape your healing?

9. **How do your self-perceptions affect your ability to connect with others?**
    Are you projecting old narratives that may no longer be true?

10. **What do you believe about your own worthiness for love, friendship, and support?**
    And are you willing to rewrite that story if it's no longer serving you?

RISE Reminders

- Healing is not meant to be a solo act. I am allowed to lean on others.
- There is strength in being seen, and courage in being known.
- My story doesn't make me too much—it makes me real, and it makes me needed.
- I am worthy of connection, even when I feel broken.
- The right people won't be repelled by my truth—they'll be drawn to it.

PART IV
EMBODY THE PURPOSE

CHAPTER 10
IT'S OKAY TO WANT MORE THAN JUST SURVIVING

There's an unspoken rule in the aftermath of trauma that no one really says out loud, but many of us absorb: **You should be grateful you survived. And that's it.** Be quiet. Be humble. Be thankful. Stay small.

Wanting *more*—joy, purpose, success, visibility, love—can feel . . . inappropriate. Selfish, even. As if survival was the ultimate prize and to ask for anything beyond it is greedy.

I remember feeling this in my bones. I had survived what many people do not. I had been pulled from the brink of death by the hands of strangers who risked their lives to bring me home. So who was I to want more?

Who was I to tell my story from the big stage? Did I deserve a platform? Could I develop a new career? I was lucky to be alive, but was I asking for too much to want a sense of fulfillment from my life complete with a new identity?

I would wake up in the middle of the night in a cold sweat wondering: *Who am I to believe I still deserve these things?*

What no one talks about is how shame can sneak in—not because of what happened to us, but because of what we begin to *desire* afterward. We're told to count our blessings. We're told that we're lucky just to be here. We're told to be thankful we got a second chance.

And yes—we are.

But if we stop there, we risk living in a self-imposed prison of low expectations. We risk becoming curators of our own smallness, rather than architects of our expansion.

Survival is sacred. But it is not the end of our story.

This was life altering for me and I wonder if it will be for you too: **You are allowed to want more.**

When I began writing more publicly, speaking (and getting paid for it!), and dreaming again—I kept bumping up against this voice that asked, *Is this allowed? Am I allowed to want meaning now? Am I allowed to want more than healing? Am I allowed to feel joy—even as I still carry grief?*

Shame whispers that your survival was already too much to ask for, so you should never ask for anything again. But here's the truth: **Survival does not cancel out your worthiness. It affirms it.**

You are not indebted to the world for the rest of your life—and I had to learn after many years, that I was not indebted to SEAL Team Six for the rest of mine. You do not have to *earn your keep* with silence, invisibility, or self-denial. You are not here just to survive— you are here to become.

At some point, I started asking different questions:

Not "What am I allowed to do now?" but **"What do I want to do now?"**

Not "Who needs me to be something for them?" but **"Who am I becoming for myself?"**

Not "How do I repay the world for saving me?" but **"How do I honor this life I've been given by living it fully?"**

It was terrifying, honestly. Because I still had one foot in the past, and I worried that moving forward meant I was abandoning the version of myself who fought so hard to stay alive, or that I would mess up my new endeavors and fail epically, therefore rendering me undeserving of survival. But I wasn't leaving her behind—I was building upon her.

There is no betrayal in wanting more. There is no shame in expanding.

If you're reading this and you've survived something that broke you open, let me say this to you now, as clearly as I can:

You are still allowed to dream.

You are still allowed to build.

You are still allowed to shine.

You do not owe the world smallness to prove that you are grateful. You do not have to downplay your gifts to make others comfortable. You do not have to stay stuck in the ashes to honor what you lost. Wanting more doesn't make you selfish. It makes you *human*.

You've already paid a high price. You've endured the unimaginable. That doesn't mean you are now exempt from ambition, or creativity, or calling. It means you are *ready* to let your life become more than what hurt you.

There is sacredness in survival. There is also sacredness in expansion. And you, my friend?

You are worthy of both.

The Risk to Rise

Every time I've stepped into something new since surviving—whether it was telling my story on a stage, launching a project, or simply showing up more fully in my life—I've felt the same knot in my stomach. A quiet, persistent question: *Is this a risk worth taking?*

And the truth is: yes. Rising always comes with risk. But maybe not the kind we think.

When we talk about risk in the aftermath of trauma, our nervous systems still equate *attention*, *visibility*, or *change* with danger. Survival made us hyperaware of what could go wrong. We learned to brace for impact by staying small, safe, and unseen.

But once we're out of the crisis, many of the risks we perceive are no longer life-or-death. They are emotional risks; psychological and social—and more often than not, imagined ones. But it doesn't matter because they *still feel real*.

Let's name some of the common "risks" survivors face when they start to rise:

"What if people think I'm self-absorbed?"

The moment you speak your story or share your truth, a little voice might whisper: *This is too much. You're making this about you.* But here's what I've learned: **There is a difference between being self-centered and being self-expressed.** You are not sharing to perform. You are sharing to connect. One of my favorite quotes of all time is: "I heal out loud so that others who are hurting in silence know it is possible." Regardless of what the haters may say (and believe me, I've got a lot of them!), sharing your powerful story is a beautiful contribution and act of service, my friend.

"What if I'm judged for profiting from my pain?"

This one is loaded, especially for those of us who speak, write, or teach from personal experience and support our families by doing so. I struggled with this for so long—and I talk about it a lot in more detail in other formats, but for the purposes of this book, I'm going to leave it right here with this truth: **Your story is not for sale—it's in service.** You're not capitalizing on your trauma. You're creating something from the ashes. And **if your work provides value to others, and sustains you in return, that is not exploitation. That is** *integration.* Stop for a moment and let that sink in. If telling your story is serving others and yourself and it does not feel imbalanced energetically, then you have successfully integrated the pain, alchemized it into an offering, a contribution for the world.

"What if I try something new and I fail?"

Failure feels catastrophic after trauma because we've already lost so much. The idea of losing more—our confidence, reputation, direction—can paralyze us. But ask yourself: **What's really at stake?** Embarrassment? Disappointment? Redirection? You've already survived the unimaginable. Starting a podcast, pitching your book, or applying for that job? That's *not* a real risk. That's a bold act of rebuilding, and you and I both know you are way more resilient than the beliefs that are holding you back.

"What if I change too much and people leave?"

Trauma has a way of rearranging who we are, and with growth, comes change. Not everyone will understand that. Some will drift. Some may no longer fit. But here's the thing: **People leaving isn't the greatest loss—staying small to keep them comfortable is.** Let the right people find you on the other side of your becoming.

"What if I get hurt again?"

Yes. That is a possibility. Vulnerability is not without risk. People might misunderstand you. A project might flop. A door might close.

But here's the question you have to ask: **What if you** *don't* **try? What if you never find out what's possible because fear told you**

it wasn't safe to dream again? The biggest risk may not be rising. It might be staying still.

So no, rising isn't without risk. But most of the "dangers" we brace for now are echoes of old survival patterns—trying to protect us from rejection, failure, or pain. And while those fears are valid, they don't get to be the architects of your future.

There is risk in rising, but there is also risk in hiding.

There is risk in dreaming, but there is also risk in settling.

There is risk in wanting more, but there is even greater risk in pretending that survival was the end of your story.

You've already faced the unimaginable. And yet, here you are— still here, still becoming.

Don't let the fear of perception keep you from stepping into your purpose.

You're not too much.

You're not ungrateful.

You're not a burden

You are *becoming*—and that is always worth the risk.

The Weight of Thriver's Guilt

We've all heard of *survivor's guilt*—the heavy grief that settles in when you make it out of something that others didn't. But what happens when you begin to not only survive . . . but actually *do well?* What happens when you start to thrive?

There's a lesser-known, equally complex feeling that begins to rise. I call it **thriver's guilt.**

It's that strange discomfort that creeps in when life starts to open up again—when opportunities arrive, when joy surprises you, when your voice begins to rise above the wreckage. It's the guilt that says, *You've already had your miracle, so why are you asking for more?*

I didn't name this phenomenon myself—*Psychology Today* describes thriver's guilt as "the feeling that emerges when someone begins to thrive in the aftermath of something traumatic or tragic, especially if others are still suffering."[8] It showed up for a lot of people during the pandemic—when some found healing, clarity, or career shifts while others were in crisis.

For me, this guilt was personal, deeply spiritual, and as is usual for me, shame-laced.

I was raised in the church—conditioned to believe that I needed to be good, humble, obedient, and above all, small. Don't shine too brightly! Don't take up too much space! Don't speak unless you're spoken to! Every impure thought, every outburst of anger, every stray emotion was to be tucked in tight, repented for, and replaced with a smile.

That wiring stays with you. It's like it becomes muscle memory and before you know what is happening, you just get sucked right back in.

So after my kidnapping and rescue, when people started to take notice of my story—when opportunities began to arise, when my name showed up on book covers and interview segments—I felt a visceral resistance. *This isn't supposed to be about me,* I thought. *This is too much. I'm too much.*

I'd sit in my therapist's office, trying to articulate the shame I couldn't quite name. It wasn't survivor's guilt—not exactly. I had grieved the lives lost during my rescue operation. I had done the painful work of releasing the guilt that came with that. I knew in my

---

8   Camille Preston, "So You Thrived in the Pandemic, Turning Guilt into Grati-tude," *Psychology Today*, July 15, 2021, https://www.psychologytoday.com/us/blog/mental-health-in-the-workplace/202107/so-you-thrived-in-the-pandemic-turning-guilt-into.

bones that I hadn't asked for this experience, and I had made peace with the decisions made far above my pay grade.

No, this was something else.

This was guilt that wrapped itself around *success*. Around *visibility*. Around the slow, steady rebuild of a life that was starting to feel full again.

Thriver's guilt whispered to me that I had already used up my miracle. That to speak up more boldly, to share more of my story, to grow my work and let my platform expand—that was greedy. That was attention-seeking.

It told me that the SEALs were the only real heroes, and that I had no right to be the one with a microphone. I was exploiting my pain, even as I worked to transform it into purpose.

And so I dimmed as I self-censored. I often sat on my story and just tried to be grateful and quiet, forgetting that two things can exist together. You can be both grateful *and* expansive.

Eventually, the guilt turned into paralysis and the anxiety kept me up at night as I waited for the other shoe to drop, or at the very least, for someone to call me out and say what I feared most: *You don't deserve this.*

Until one day, I found myself asking a different question: **Is this what the SEALs rescued me for?**

Did they risk their lives in the middle of the night, drop out of the sky into enemy territory, walk through the desert with the weight of war on their backs . . . so that I could survive, but never *live?*

No.

They didn't rescue me so I could shrink.

They rescued me so I could rise.

So I could *thrive*—guilt-free.

That moment in my therapist's office was a shift. The clouds didn't clear all at once, but the air got lighter. I walked out of there with a new commitment to myself:

I would stop apologizing for healing; I would stop asking permission to shine.

I would stop dimming my voice so others wouldn't feel uncomfortable.

Because thriving isn't betrayal; it's bravery, and I had earned every inch of this life.

Survivor Spotlight: Jamie Metcalf—Learning to Live Again

For a long time after her husband David died by suicide, Jamie Metcalf lived with the aching sense that everything she did was somehow wrong.

David, a decorated Navy SEAL, had returned home from years of intense service with invisible wounds—ones that even Jamie, his closest companion, hadn't fully seen. He died by suicide six years ago, after nearly twenty years of service, a career that had once defined him.

His death blindsided her. Not just because it was sudden—but because it didn't match the man she knew. She told me, "I thought I was a bad wife because I didn't see the signs."

In the military culture they had lived in, mental health and suicide were still treated as weaknesses. Silence was the unspoken rule. That made her grief not only overwhelming—but confusing and isolating. In order to make sense of everything, Jamie kept trying to put herself in David's shoes, retracing every step, trying to understand what he had carried, and what she had missed.

In those early years, Jamie searched for validation through service; she threw herself into speaking events, military support groups, and veteran memorials, telling David's story again and again, hoping that by keeping his legacy alive, she could honor him enough to quiet the ache of regret, and maybe help other service members and their families too.

She asked herself, constantly, *What would David want me to do?*

But with every speech and every conversation, she felt herself wearing thin. She was giving everything to preserve his memory—and leaving nothing for her own healing.

After a Veteran's Day memorial, in which she had to travel far away from her son to speak in front of a large crowd, Jamie realized she had been focusing so much on David's death, she had forgotten how to live. She was surviving—but she wasn't living.

And beneath it all, there was another weight many survivors know well but rarely name: the guilt of continuing on. Jamie felt guilty for smiling again, laughing and dreaming.

The guilt of imagining a life beyond the loss of David felt insurmountable, but she woke up one morning and looked at her son and realized she didn't want to just wake up every day and say she was only living for the sake of his well-being, even though for a long time, that's all she felt she was allowed to do.

Eventually, and thanks to life-saving therapy that included many sessions of EMDR, Jamie began to ask a different question—not, *What would David want me to do?* But rather, *What do I want to do?*

She realized that surviving David's death didn't mean she had to stay in the shadow of it, and that it was okay to want more. It was okay to build a life that honored him *and* brought her joy, so that she could move forward—not because she was moving on, but because she was *choosing life*, for her and her son. And it didn't matter what anyone else had to say about it.

After much time spent in prayer and contemplation, Jamie returned to something that had always brought her peace—using her hands to help others heal. She saw clearly that God had given her the gift of touch, and so she enrolled in school to become a medical massage therapist, with a vision of working with veterans who, like David, carry trauma in their bodies they don't always know how to speak out loud.

She's still walking her path—still raising her son, still learning what it means to rebuild a life that holds space for grief, healing, and hope. She drives one hour and forty-five minutes one way to attend her classes, is the primary caregiver for her son, and thinks about David every minute of every day.

She told me: "We're going to grieve every day, but it matures—and you mature in the way you grieve. That helps us look at life differently."

And when she feels that old guilt creep in, she remembers what her son—now eight years old—told her not long ago:

"Life is just life. So just smile."

How Jamie's Story Reflects the RISE Framework
R – Reckon with the Pain
Jamie didn't run from her grief, she confronted the crushing shock of David's death, the confusion around how it happened, and the belief that somehow it was her fault.

She lived in the questions and sat with the silence. She felt it all—raw and real.

I – Identify the Impact

Jamie began to understand how deeply David's death had shaped her—not just emotionally, but in how she saw herself, her worth, and her role in the world.

She identified the patterns of guilt and the need for external validation that kept her stuck in performance rather than healing.

S – Seek the Meaning

When the speaking engagements stopped filling her up, Jamie began looking inward.

She asked what David's legacy could become if she carried it forward *in a way that also nourished her*. She saw that her own life, her own healing, could be part of that legacy.

E – Embody the Purpose

Now, through her training as a medical massage therapist, Jamie is building something lasting—something that serves the veteran community and honors David's memory in a way that is grounded in service and filled with love. She's using the pain that once threatened to consume her as a bridge to help others heal.

Jamie's story shows us that thriving after loss isn't betrayal—it's bravery, and that guilt often lingers not because we've done something wrong, but because we're learning to believe we're worthy of joy again. Healing doesn't mean we forget; it means we choose to keep living *with* the memory, *not under* it.

What I've Learned About Surviving Thriver's Guilt

1. **Gratitude is the grounding force**

   I used gratitude to stay sane in captivity, and I use it now to stay centered in freedom. Every night, I listed five things I was thankful for—even if one of them was, *"I still have my toenails."* The same practice helps me when guilt creeps in. I remind myself where I've been, and how far I've come.

2. **Other people's opinions don't get to run my life**

   Not everyone will understand what I've been through or what I'm building. That's okay. My life doesn't need to be explained to anyone. I stopped outsourcing my worthiness.

3. **I give back because I want to—not to prove I deserve my life**

   Giving is part of my nature. But now I do it from a place of overflow, not obligation.

4. **I speak about it—unapologetically**

   Shame thrives in silence. So I started talking about thriver's guilt. And surprise—other people felt it too. Naming it helped dissolve it.

If you're carrying this kind of guilt, let me tell you something I wish I had heard earlier:

You are allowed to thrive.

You are not selfish.

You are not stealing attention.

You are not ungrateful.

You are *becoming*.

And that? That is what you were rescued for.

PAUSE, PONDER, AND PROCESS RELEASING THRIVER'S GUILT AND THE COURAGE TO WANT MORE

1. **Where in your life have you felt like you needed to apologize for doing well?**
   What was the story behind that guilt?

2. **Have you ever felt that your healing or growth made others uncomfortable?**
   How did that influence your choices?

3. **What beliefs were you raised with about humility, attention, or success?**
   How might those beliefs be showing up in your healing?

4. **When have you dimmed your light in order to protect someone else's comfort?**
   How did that affect your own growth?

5. **What does thriving look like for you now—and what would it take to step fully into it?**

6. **Who do you fear will judge you if you succeed?**
   Are those people truly part of your healing journey?

7. **What would it feel like to give yourself full permission to thrive—without guilt or justification?**

8. **What have you been taught—explicitly or subtly—about what you're "allowed" to want after trauma? Or in general, for that matter?**
   How is that shaping your beliefs today?

9. **Do you ever feel guilt or shame for wanting more from life, even after everything you've been through?**
   Where do those feelings come from?

10. **In what areas of your life are you holding back out of fear that others will judge you for shining or succeeding?**

11. **What would "wanting more" look like for you right now?**
    More joy, more purpose, more peace, more visibility?

12. **Have you been waiting for permission to grow, to create, or to speak up?**
    What if that permission had to come from *you*?

13. **What story have you been telling yourself about your worthiness—and is it still true?**

14. **What would it look like to expand without guilt?**
    Who might benefit from your courage to live out loud?

RISE Reminders: You're Allowed to Thrive

- I don't have to apologize for surviving—and I definitely don't have to apologize for living.
- Thriving doesn't mean I've forgotten what I've been through. It means I've honored it with growth.
- I am not selfish for wanting more. I am healing out loud.
- Gratitude grounds me. Guilt does not define me.
- My thriving is not a threat. It's an invitation—for others to rise too.
- The miracle wasn't just my rescue. It's my ability to keep becoming.

CHAPTER 11
HEALING OUT LOUD

One of the questions people ask me the most is if I ever got to meet the SEALs after my rescue. It's hard to believe, but no, I did not. They all just faded into the dark night, because that is what they do. They save lives and our country, anonymously, without us even knowing how they do it or who they are.

However, over the past several years, I have gotten to meet and become friends with several SEALs and members of the SEAL community—which has been an incredibly rewarding experience.

The very first time I ever stood in front of an audience to tell my story, mostly focused on the rescue, was at an event sponsored by the Navy SEAL Foundation, an organization that I have been associated with for years that supports the families of active duty and fallen SEALs. It was a multiday golfing event, and they had me scheduled for the final keynote after dinner. Prior to standing in front of a crowd of hundreds of people, I went to go get my hair done at the salon at the hotel (it didn't turn out very well, she had me looking like a younger version of Barbara Bush toward the end!), but what happened while I was in the chair will always stay with me—and not in a good way.

I was minding my own business, flipping through a magazine and nervously watching the disaster of a blowout unfolding in the salon mirror when I noticed the woman seated next to me, getting her hair done for the same event. Actually, I heard her before I noticed her, because, quite frankly, she was loud and was talking a lot. It was clear that she was the wife of one of the SEALs in attendance, and I was hoping to get out of there before she recognized me. Alas, it would not be so, and about halfway through our individual hair curling sessions, she looked at me in the mirror and gasped, "Are you Jessica Buchanan?" I blushed, watching color creep up my neck and settle under my curled up bangs as I struggled with the temptation to deny it.

"Yes . . ." I responded quietly, meeting her eyes in the beauty salon mirror. She freaked out, quite literally.

I'm not sure what the driving emotion was for her, but what I remember from that encounter is one of the things she said to me: "Do you even know how many of those guys who went out to rescue you had pregnant wives waiting for them at home?"

I didn't know. But at that moment, I was completely overwhelmed with shame. All I could do was shake my head.

And as she kept talking, and telling me all about the wives of these great men that did indeed risk their lives to save mine, my guilt began to grow until I thought I might either suffocate or have a panic attack right there in front of her.

That night, I shared the story of how I had been out there for ninety-three days and was beginning to doubt that I was going to survive. The retelling was very well received, and they were able to raise millions of dollars for the foundation. Not because of me, but because of the amazing work these men do, as well as the families that support them.

However, without knowing it, I made a deal with the narrative that I was going to share from that point on: me, the damsel in distress; the SEALs, my knights in shining armour.

* * *

Several years ago, I was speaking for the SEAL Legacy Foundation at their annual fundraising gala in Dallas. This is a different organization than the Navy SEAL Foundation. I had come to find out that there were several organizations supporting the SEALs and their families, which was great. I was teaching at the time, but feeling that compulsion to find something different; my intuition was telling me there was something more deeply connected to my purpose for me to do, but I couldn't figure out what it was. When I finished speaking, as is the case most of the time, a few people came up to me afterwards to ask questions—one of them had a very important connection, and he had a question for me that would change the trajectory of my healing journey.

"Would you like to meet the SEALs that rescued you?" He asked me, after introducing himself as a board member of the foundation. He also happened to be closely related to the commanding officer of SEAL Team Six at the time.

I didn't even blink, but rather blurted out "YES!" in his face. He took my information, and didn't make any promises, but was fairly sure he could make something happen relatively soon.

It took nearly six months, but finally, I got word that a meeting with Naval Special Warfare Development Group (DEVGRU) had been arranged and that the SEALs who were able and still active, as well as some who were no longer active but had been on my rescue mission, were ready to gather in Virginia Beach to meet me, again.

I didn't know what to think. I didn't know how to feel. I was nervous and scared; excited and quiet.

My best friend from childhood, who is still my best friend today, called me up a few days before I was to drive down for the reunion and offered to join me for moral support. I declined her offer at first, but after thinking about it for a little while, decided maybe I *did* need someone to go with me and just hold space for me at such an important moment in my life.

We booked a hotel room by the ocean and slept with the door open all night so we could be lulled to sleep by the waves of the Atlantic.

I hardly slept, rehearsing everything I wanted to be sure I said to them. This was my one shot to make sure they knew how grateful I was. There was a lot riding on this meeting for me.

Unable to keep my breakfast down, I was so nervous, I could barely think straight. I'm not sure now, in retrospect, what I was so nervous about, but I think it was the impending emotional release I knew was coming. I knew it was necessary, but also could feel that it was going to be incredibly draining. I think there was a lot of fear for me too, going into this "reunion." What if I didn't measure up? What if they didn't approve of how I was living my life? What if I hadn't done enough to deem myself worthy of them risking their lives so that I could live? What if they all thought I was just a total waste of their mission? The SEAL's wife's words from the beauty shop encounter kept bouncing around inside my head: "Do you even know . . . ???" That's a lot to carry around, and I was exhausted from having carried around those shameful thoughts for the last several years. I didn't realize just how much I needed to lay them down.

My host picked me up at the hotel and I hugged my best friend goodbye and promised to call when I could. I had to leave my phone in the car, and nervously followed him into an office building decorated in all sorts of SEAL Team memorabilia. My picture was one of the first ones to grace the hallway leading to the conference room where I would meet my saviors.

As soon as I walked into the room, I noticed how long the conference table was. It seemed like it stretched on for miles, and at it, dozens of America's most elite soldiers were seated. I did not recognize a single one of them—it was so dark that night and I was in so much shock—how could I?

They all rose and waited quietly and respectfully as I walked into the room and took my place at the head of the table, it was the only empty chair. And then, I burst into tears.

All this time had passed, and I didn't realize how badly I needed to connect with them, because I had something very important to say: THANK YOU.

For the ones that were there that night, we walked through the entire mission, step by step, filling in blanks for each other. I got answers to questions I had long held and surrendered to never getting answered. I sobbed as I told them about my children, and that I was working very hard to live a life of meaning and purpose. I wanted to make them proud.

At the end of a very long, and exhausting, yet profoundly impactful day, we stood out front and said our final goodbyes. The SEAL who was the first to make point of contact with me on that night in January, the one who told me I was finally safe, and that they were going to take me home, gave me one final hug and changed my life, yet again, when he said, "You know, Jess, you think we are the heroes here, but you had to survive those ninety-three days when you didn't think anyone was coming for you. That's some tough stuff. I hope you know what a badass we think you are."

Instead of crying (this time!), I stood a little taller and humbly accepted his observation. I let it settle inside my heart, driving out the shame that had taken up residence inside me. I had been telling the story, being very careful to make sure that people understood I was the damsel in distress and they were the heroes who had come in to save the day. And while all of that is true, they did come in and save the day, along with my life—and in a major way—what I learned in that moment, and it really is the most life changing lesson I have learned when it relates to how I tell my story and how I view myself, is: there can be more than one hero. They are certainly outstanding. But, I can be one too.

The Power of Telling Our Stories

There's something profoundly human about the need to tell our stories, especially the ones forged in pain. For those of us carrying emotional trauma, the simple yet brave act of putting our experiences into words, whether through speaking or writing, can become a powerful path to healing.

Science backs up what so many survivors intuitively know: when we give voice to the things we've carried silently, the burden lightens. Dr. James Pennebaker, a pioneer in the study of expressive writing, found that people who wrote about their trauma for just fifteen to twenty minutes a day over several days experienced significant improvements in both physical and mental health.[9] They visited doctors less often because they felt less anxious and depressed. Some studies showed that PTSD symptoms decreased by as much as 40 percent. And it wasn't just a short-term fix—the benefits lingered.

This is because writing helps us process and organize what once felt chaotic. Trauma often lives in the body and the unspoken corners of our minds. But when we write it down, we begin to understand it—to give it shape and meaning. It becomes a story, not just a wound. Speaking our truth carries its own unique magic. In the context of therapy, support groups, or simply heartfelt conversations, verbal storytelling invites connection. We are seen, heard, and sometimes, gently mirrored back to ourselves with empathy. In trauma-focused group therapy, participants have shown symptom reductions as high as 60–70 percent. These aren't just numbers; they represent lives changed by the simple act of being witnessed.

There's also something fascinating happening in the brain. Neuroimaging has shown that storytelling activates not just our language centers, but also the regions responsible for emotion and memory. When we tell our stories, we're literally rewiring the way our brains hold trauma. Cortisol levels drop. Oxytocin, the hormone tied to trust and emotion, rises. This isn't just catharsis; it's chemistry.

Some people find solace in writing first, when the feelings are still too raw to speak out loud. Others find strength in immediately reaching out, using their voice to push back the silence. There's no right way to begin—only that we do begin. And often, the most powerful healing happens when we use both: writing to untangle our inner world and speaking to connect with others who say, "Me too."

---

9   Louise DeSalvo, *Writing as a Way of Healing: How Telling Our Stories Transforms Our Lives* (Beacon Press, 2000).

Telling your story doesn't mean reliving your pain. It means reclaiming it because we are able to turn something that once overwhelmed us into something we now hold in our hands. You become the author, not just the survivor, because what's shareable becomes bearable. And what's spoken or written with honesty and courage becomes a bridge—one that leads not just back to ourselves, but forward, into something new.

When we share our story, especially the parts we've spent years hiding, grieving, or trying to forget, we do something revolutionary. We offer others not just our pain, but our humanity. We say: "You're not alone." And sometimes, that's exactly what someone else needs to hear to keep going.

Our Stories Become Bridges

When we share our stories, what was once a private scar becomes a shared truth. And suddenly, someone out there who thought they were the only one struggling realizes there's someone who understands. That connection—soul to soul—is healing in itself.

It's not about having a happy ending. It's about showing the courage it takes to keep walking through the mess. Sharing our story invites others to do the same. We become mirrors, showing them their strength too.

But here's the other piece, which is so relevant to the reason for which I have spent months writing this book: when we speak our truth, we connect to our *why*.

One post, speech, workshop, conversation can help us remember that we didn't survive for nothing and shows us that our wounds have shaped us—not defined us—and maybe, just maybe, they've carved space for a purpose bigger than our pain.

In telling our stories, we reclaim them, and in reclaiming them, we begin to rewrite them, not just for ourselves, but for anyone still searching for hope in the darkness of their pain. When we speak the truth of who we are, we don't just heal ourselves, we light the way for others to come home to themselves too.

Just as I began to find the courage to tell my story, incorporating this new narrative that I could be a hero too, something unexpected crept in—a quiet but persistent voice whispering, *Who do you think you are?* Of course, imposter syndrome showed up, right on cue. At first, it sounded like concern. *Other people have been through worse. You're not healed enough. You're not a writer.* But under the surface, it was fear; fear of being seen, of getting it wrong, of being told that my story didn't matter.

Imposter syndrome is clever like that. It disguises itself as humility, as logic, as realism. But really, it's just your inner critic panicking because you're daring to do something brave.

Here's what I've learned: the moment you start to speak your truth is often the exact moment that voice shows up the loudest. And not because you're a fraud, but because what you're doing *matters*. Sharing your story shakes something loose in the world. It challenges shame. It disrupts silence. That's powerful. And power often attracts resistance.

But here's the deeper truth—**you don't need permission to tell your story.** You don't need a title, a degree, a perfect ending, or a flawless draft. You lived it. You felt it. You survived it. That alone makes you worthy of telling it.

People don't connect with perfection; they connect with *truth*. They feel seen when you share your humanness. You don't have to be a finished product to offer something real. In fact, you don't have to be "healed" to be helpful. Sometimes the most powerful stories come from the middle of the journey, not the end. And when you feel unsure—which you will, believe me, after twelve years of telling my own story, I sometimes do—just come back to your *why*. Ask yourself: *Are you sharing to heal? Are you sharing to be free?*

Do you think your story can help someone else feel less alone? If the answer is yes, then be assured that your purpose—your *why*— is stronger than any doubt.

Sometimes we need to borrow belief, maybe from a friend, a therapist, a mentor, until we remember our own. But even if no one else speaks into your courage today, let me:

You are not an imposter. You are a survivor. A truth-teller. A light-holder. Your story may not be for everyone. But it will be everything to someone.

And that is more than enough.

Seven Steps to Start Sharing Your Story

1. **Start with your *why***

   Ask yourself: *Why do I want to share my story?*

   Is it to heal? To help others? To understand yourself better?

   Your why becomes an anchor—something to come back to when the process feels overwhelming or uncertain.

2. **Begin in a safe, private space (writing is a great first step)**

   Start by journaling, even if it's messy, raw, or fragmented. Let it flow without worrying about grammar, structure, or judgment. This is for your eyes only—a way to open the door gently.

   Here are a couple prompts to try:

- What do I wish someone knew about what I went through?
- What would I say to my younger self at that moment?

3. Choose one part of your story to begin with

You don't have to start at the beginning. You don't have to tell it all. Choose a memory, a turning point, or a feeling. Starting small helps build trust with yourself—and makes the process feel more manageable.

4. Honor your boundaries

You're in control of your story so you get to decide what you're ready to share—and what needs to stay private for now. Healing isn't about forcing exposure, it's about choosing what feels right.

It's okay to say: "That part's not ready to be shared yet."

5. Speak it out loud (even just to yourself)

Read your words back to yourself. Say them in a mirror. Hear how they sound in your own voice. This helps shift the story from something locked inside to something you can begin to carry with awareness and compassion.

6. Share with someone you trust

When you feel ready, open up to a trusted friend, therapist, or support group. Choose someone who can listen without judgment or trying to fix you. Feeling heard and validated is incredibly healing. *Reminder:* The goal isn't to impress. It's to be real.

7. **Find your rhythm and your medium**

    Some people write books. Others speak at support groups,
    post on social media, start podcasts, write poetry, or create art.
    There's no one right way. The best way is the one that feels
    most *you*.

Sharing your story doesn't require perfection or eloquence,
only honesty and heart. You're not just telling what happened; you're
reclaiming your voice, shaping your truth, and maybe, just maybe,
lighting the path for someone else.

Survivor Spotlight: Sam Goodwin—Your Pain Can Become Your Prison or Your Platform

In 2019, Sam Goodwin was close to achieving a remarkable personal
goal: visiting every country in the world.

A former college hockey player turned global traveler, Sam was
driven by curiosity, connection, and a deep belief in the goodness of
people.

When he entered Syria—one of the final countries on his
list—he knew there were risks.

But what he didn't know was that within hours of his arrival,
his life would be changed forever.

Sam was kidnapped at gunpoint and thrown into a secret
Syrian prison. Accused of being a spy, stripped of communication
with the outside world, and kept in brutal conditions, he spent
sixty-two terrifying days in captivity. He was interrogated, isolated,
and completely cut off from his family, who had no idea where he
was or if he was even alive.

During those long days and nights, Sam faced the unthinkable:
the possibility that he might never leave, the temptation to lose

hope, and the challenge of surviving not just physically, but mentally and spiritually. I can identify with that pain.

Through it all, he held onto something deeper—a stubborn will to survive, a connection to his faith, and an unwavering belief that somehow, his life still had purpose beyond that prison cell.

And against incredible odds, diplomatic negotiations, largely led by Lebanese officials, secured Sam's release. He returned home not just carrying the weight of his survival, but carrying the even bigger question: *How do you live after you've lived through something like that?*

Instead of hiding, Sam chose to tell his story. Sam's memoir, *Saving Sam: The True Story of an American's Disappearance in Syria and His Family's Extraordinary Fight to Bring Him Home*, was published in 2024, and it is an excellent retelling that chronicles his experience and the lessons he learned in captivity.

Sam began speaking publicly about resilience, hope, and the unbreakable parts of the human spirit because he felt like he had a responsibility to share what he had learned about the human spirit and resilience. He felt like he had survived in order to help other people with his story, and he told me over coffee not too long ago that his prayer, every time he goes on stage is: "Please help me help one person. And occasionally, let me know who it is." When this happens, Sam says it is a reminder that he is exactly where he needs to be.

Today, Sam's story is not just about what happened to him; it's about what he chose to do next.

It's about how he turned pain into a platform—and how sharing our stories can be a profound part of healing, for ourselves and for others.

How Sam's Story Reflects the RISE Framework

Sam's journey is a vivid reminder that surviving the moment of crisis is only part of the story.

The deeper survival—the survival of the spirit, the rebuilding of identity—comes when we find the courage to reclaim and tell our story.

Sam's life reflects the RISE framework in powerful, deeply human ways:

R – Reckon with the Pain

Sam didn't deny what had happened to him. He faced the trauma of captivity head-on—the fear, the disorientation, the grief for the version of his life that was lost. Writing *Saving Sam* was part of that reckoning: telling the full truth, not just the easy parts.

I – Identify the Impact

Sam recognized that his experience had forever changed him and so he didn't try to "go back" to who he was before Syria. He understood that the impact was real and lasting—and that surviving survival would mean integrating those changes, not ignoring them.

S – Seek the Meaning

Rather than letting his story remain a private wound, Sam sought to create meaning from his experience. He asked bigger questions about purpose, faith, and the resilience of the human spirit through his writing and speaking. He transformed his pain into a message of hope and perseverance for others and that legacy will live on for a very long time.

E – Embody the Purpose

Today, Sam's storytelling extends far beyond his personal healing. By sharing openly, he helps others understand resilience in a new way. As he offers fellow survivors—of all kinds—a map for how pain can become a platform, a way to connect, to heal, and to inspire.

Sam's story reminds us that pain, by itself, is not the end. It's what we choose to build from that pain that determines the legacy we leave behind. Telling our stories—courageously, truthfully, imperfectly—is one of the most powerful ways we survive survival.

PAUSE, PONDER, AND PROCESS

1. **Ground into Your Story**
   These prompts help you begin where you are, without needing to relive everything at once.

   – *Right now, I feel . . .*
   Free write for ten minutes about your current emotional state. Let it be unfiltered.

   – *If my pain had a voice, it would say . . .*
   What would your trauma or pain tell you if it could speak?

   – *A moment that changed everything was . . .*
   Describe it with as many sensory details as possible. What did you see, hear, feel?

   – *I've never told anyone that . . .*
   This is a private space. Be gentle, but honest. You can rip it up or delete it later if needed.

   – *The part of my story I avoid is . . .*
   Write about why you avoid it—not the story itself yet. What emotions are there?

2. **Reclaim the Narrative**
   This section helps you reflect and regain a sense
   of control and authorship.

   – *If I could go back to that version of myself, I
   would say . . .*
   Write a letter to your past self in the moment of
   pain or confusion.

   – *What I survived taught me . . .*
   Explore the wisdom or strength you've gained—
   even if it's still unfolding.

   – *I'm still learning how to . . .*
   Healing isn't linear. What are you still figuring
   out? Give yourself grace.

   – *My healing looks like . . .*
   Paint a picture of your healing—literally or
   figuratively. Is it a garden, a sunrise, a scar?

   – *I want to tell my story because . . .*
   Reconnect with your purpose. This can be the
   start of a speech, a memoir, or just for you.

3. **Write to Be Heard**
   These prompts help shape your story for sharing—with others or even the world.

   – *If I could tell the world one truth, it would be . . .*
   What's the essence of what you want others to
   understand?

   – *Here's what I've learned about silence . . .*
   Reflect on what staying silent has meant—and
   what breaking that silence might offer.

   – *The hardest part to say out loud is . . .*
   Name it. Even if you don't write the details yet.

> – *Someone else out there needs to hear . . .*
> Write as if you're speaking to someone who's been where you've been.
>
> – *I'm not just my pain. I'm also . . .*
> Remind yourself—and others—of your full humanity.

RISE Reminders: When It Feels Too Much

- Right now, I'm safe. I'm here. And in this moment, I choose to . . .

Survivor Spotlight: Mollie McGuire—A New Definition of Justice

Mollie McGuire spent her career fighting for children. As a child abuse prosecutor in Chicago, she carried the stories of kids whose pain had been ignored, silenced, or swept under the rug. She understood the law, she understood trauma, and she believed—fiercely—in the systems meant to protect the most vulnerable.

But nothing prepared her for the moment those systems failed her own child.

At the time, Mollie was the mother of three boys—her oldest was in first grade when the panic attacks started. At first, it was subtle. He was anxious, yes, but he was also whip-smart. The kind of smart that gets misunderstood in the traditional classroom. The school chalked up his behavior to defiance or distraction. But by second grade, things escalated.

Her son was eventually diagnosed with autism and severe anxiety. But before that diagnosis came, there were moments that still make Mollie's voice catch in her throat: finding him face-down on the classroom floor, soaked in sweat from a panic attack. Watching him retreat further and further from the world. Hearing him repeat, again and again, that he wasn't safe at school.

So they pulled him out. And when they requested his school records, what they found was beyond disturbing. Internal messages between school staff described moments where he had stopped breathing—and they weren't sure whether or not to call 911. At one point, he had been placed in a closet, alone, during a medical crisis.

"I was a child abuse prosecutor," Mollie said, "and I still couldn't protect my own baby."

The trauma rippled out. Her young son began to suffer from severe depression and PTSD. He developed an eating disorder. He would binge eat before and after school to avoid the sensory overwhelm of eating in the cafeteria. Eventually, he told his parents he would rather die than talk about what was happening at school.

There was a stretch of time where Mollie said it felt like her son *had* died. He stopped talking. He wouldn't leave the house. He had to be re-potty trained. She didn't recognize him—or herself. The high-profile career woman who once fought in courtrooms was now spending her days trying to get her son to eat three bites of food.

And yet, there were glimmers.

Going to the porch. Then the playground. Adding one more food to a diet of Goldfish crackers and strawberries. These were the new milestones. And they were hard-won.

Mollie's pain cracked something open in her. She had to grieve—not just her child's suffering, but the identity she had built for herself as someone who thought she understood the system. Someone who thought she could outwork injustice.

"I had to redefine what justice looked like," she said. "It wasn't going to come in the form of a lawsuit. It was going to come through sharing our story and making things better for the next family."

So that's what she did.

Mollie is now a board member in the fourth-largest school district in the country. She advocates for children with invisible disabilities, especially those in underserved schools. She's met with legislators, done interviews with CNN, and continues to raise awareness about how reactive our education system is—and how desperately it needs reform to protect the most vulnerable students.

Three of her children now have autism diagnoses. And while this journey has turned her life upside down, it's also deepened her capacity for empathy, redefined her priorities, and given her a new understanding of purpose.

"When I think about purpose," she said, "I think about choosing to use the lessons we've learned—and the pain we've gone through—to ease other people's pain."

Her number one prayer has always been healing. Not revenge. Not control. Just healing.

And lately, healing has started to look like something she didn't expect: laughter. She recently signed up for a comedy class. Last week, she performed her first solo stand-up show.

It wasn't what she pictured when she thought of justice. But in this new chapter, joy itself is a kind of rebellion. And using your voice, even when it shakes, is one of the bravest forms of advocacy there is.

She saw how the trauma impacted her entire family system—her son's regression, his PTSD and eating disorder, and her own identity shift from courtroom advocate to full-time caregiver.

How Mollie's Story Reflects the RISE Framework

Mollie's story is about redefining justice after personal trauma. Her journey moves through grief, identity loss, and advocacy: from fighting for her son's survival to helping other families navigate invisible disabilities.

R – Reckon with the Pain

Reckoning began with the devastating realization that the very systems she trusted—schools, legal protections, the frameworks she had dedicated her career to defending—had failed her own son. Accepting this truth wasn't just about acknowledging her child's suffering; it required a complete shift in her own identity. No longer the child abuse prosecutor who fought for others in the courtroom, she was now a mother in crisis, navigating unfamiliar terrain with no clear path forward. Mourning took many forms: grieving not only her son's regression, PTSD, and eating disorder, but also the loss of her sense of control and professional purpose. Witnessing her son's isolation, watching him retreat into silence and survival, forced her to see how deeply trauma had rippled through their entire family, not just in obvious ways, but in quieter, more lasting fractures.

I – Identify the Impact

As the fog of immediate crisis began to lift, Mollie was able to look more clearly at the impact this journey had on her life. She realized that all the hard work, all the legal knowledge, all the courtroom victories she once valued—none of it had been enough to shield her family. That painful truth changed her priorities. What once felt like professional triumphs now seemed small compared to the fragile, hard-won milestones of helping her son walk out to the porch or eat a single new food. Through this process, her understanding of justice expanded. It wasn't just about law or punishment anymore; it became about empathy, healing, and quiet, patient advocacy. The experience didn't just reshape her work; it reshaped who she was, deepening her compassion and forcing her to redefine what advocacy really means.

S – Seek the Meaning

Out of necessity and heartbreak, Mollie made the choice to share her family's story. Not to invite pity, but to create change for others walking similar paths. Her search for meaning led her to a seat on her local school board, to legislative advocacy, and to speaking publicly about invisible disabilities in children. In sharing her family's truth, she redefined justice—not as revenge or legal wins, but as healing, for her family and for others. In an unexpected twist, part of that healing took the form of stand-up comedy. Reclaiming her voice through laughter gave her a surprising sense of agency and reminded her that healing can be messy, creative, and even joyful. It wasn't the kind of justice she had envisioned in her earlier life, but it was the justice her family needed.

E – Embody the Purpose

Today, Mollie embodies her purpose not through courtrooms, but through community leadership and advocacy. She uses her lived experience to help shape policy, support other families navigating school systems, and raise awareness about children with invisible disabilities. Alongside public service, she balances her own healing through humor, storytelling, and connection. Mollie's life now models what it means to rise after trauma: holding both grief and joy, seeking both justice and compassion, standing as living proof that a voice—especially one shaped by pain—can become a powerful form of rebellion and change. Her story reminds others that using your voice, even when it shakes, can offer purpose in the aftermath of loss.

PAUSE, PONDER, AND PROCESS

1. Where in your own life have you had to let go of control and trust a new definition of justice or healing?

2. What part of your identity shifted as a result of a painful experience?

3. Who might be waiting for you to use your voice—even if it feels shaky?

RISE Reminders:

- I am allowed to grow beyond the systems that once defined me.
- My voice is part of the healing, not just for me, but for others.
- Even in the aftermath, I can choose purpose over silence.

CHAPTER 12
COMMIT TO YOUR PURPOSE

There's a quiet moment in the healing journey when survival stops being the main goal.

You wake up one morning and realize that you're not fighting for your life anymore, but rather, you're fighting for your *aliveness*. The raw, aching, soul-deep kind of life that's not just about *not dying*, but about *deeply living*.

And that's when a new question starts to rise: *Now that I'm still here . . . what will I do with my life?*

That question haunted me for a long time. Not in the big, romantic, destiny-driven way—but in the day-to-day, soul-whispering way. It showed up in quiet pockets: while washing dishes, rocking my baby in the middle of the night, or waiting backstage before a talk. *What now, Jess? What matters most to you?*

I toyed around with all sorts of experimentation, as I've shared in the previous chapters, but nothing stuck. Because here's the thing I have learned: once again, it takes time. It takes curiosity, and a willingness to try, even if it's not everyday.

Eventually, I found the answer (for me)—the one that grounded me, healed me, and held me steady through the messy middle of surviving survival: purpose.

But that wasn't a job that earned me a title. I did not have a perfect plan or a perfect house or the most current car or clothes or stain-free children. But despite all that, I made a commitment to showing up, on purpose, for what mattered most; my next chapter.

There's a truth we don't talk about enough: trauma strips away the illusion of forever.

It snaps time into fragments, reminding us that everything—*everything*—can change in a moment. When you've stared down death, or you have lost what you felt was your reason for living, and then by some miracle you emerge from the rubble, you realize you have no energy left to keep chasing approval. When the dust settles and you feel you can start to wrap your brain around maybe sticking around, your appetite for the temporary, the surface, the kitchen renovations and where everyone's kids are going to college, tastes stale in the back of your mouth because what you are craving is *meaning*. You no longer have the luxury of living on autopilot, hovering above the surface of what it means to be human. And because you have met yourself, and made a pact with your soul to not just exist—you decide you want your life, your work, your essence to *matter*.

And that decision is what makes purpose not just a nice idea, but a survival skill.

When people ask me how I survived those ninety-three days, they expect me to say something tactical or brave or dramatic like, "I was amazingly observant and so knew when I could ask for food and when to stay silent." Or, "I lied and told them I was a mother, so they would understand that I had a child to get back to."

But the truth is simpler and far more sacred: I stayed alive because I believed there was still something left for me to do when I got out of there. Even in my darkest moments, I held onto the belief that there was still something in me that hadn't yet been offered to the world. There was still a story, a lesson, a conversation, a calling. And if I could hold on until morning, maybe I'd get the chance to live it. I did that day, after day, after day.

Purpose is what tethered me to life when everything else was slipping through my fingers like desert sand. But here's the hard part, and where we so often struggle: purpose doesn't land fully formed. It doesn't arrive gift-wrapped. It has to be pursued, unearthed, and committed to. Purpose grows when you stop waiting to feel "ready," and you start saying yes to the small nudges that whisper, *This. This matters. Try here. Speak here. Serve here.*

I took discovering my purpose as seriously as I did my desert survival. It felt essential to living, to breathing. I would wake up in the middle of the night, begging God to just "show me what to do!" I promised, no matter what it was, that I would do it because I couldn't waste my pain. I couldn't walk away from my survival without building something beautiful in its wake.

So I started showing up.

One journal entry, one badly written blog post, one exciting conversation with a new mom friend, eventually, one podcast episode, and then a mastermind, at a time.

Brick by brick, my purpose began to take shape—not because I figured it out in one divine epiphany, but because I committed to building it *before* I knew what it was going to look like.

Here's what I want you to know:

Committing to your purpose is the final, most courageous act of surviving survival.

It's what transforms pain into meaning, and turns you from a survivor into a guide.

Committing to your purpose is what rewrites your story from something that happened *to* you into something that moves *through* you so you can go on to share the lessons you have learned, the mountains you have climbed.

You don't have to know the full picture yet. You just have to say: *I'm here. I'm ready. Use me.*

* * *

My husband and I are not perfectionists. So it befuddles me to realize that we made one. Our youngest is that double-edged sword of inspiration and frustration: a competitive perfectionist. And I think I've said more times in the last couple of years than I thought was possible: "It doesn't have to be perfect! Just get it done!"

It's the same way with purpose; it doesn't ask you to be perfect, but rather, it asks you to just be willing. It asks you to risk being seen, being misunderstood, being changed. It asks you to let go of who you were *before it all fell apart*—so you can become who you were always meant to be. *That is the whole point!* If I could stand from every rooftop and scream this out into the world, I would.

Purpose says: *This was never just about survival. This was always about becoming.* And the moment you commit to it—not casually, not conditionally, but *wholeheartedly*—is the moment survival becomes something sacred, not something to be feared. Can you imagine what it would feel like to stop running from what happened? What freedom it would be to stop needing to explain or defend your pain to the people who have no right to judge you or your experience?

When you start standing in the truth of your life, knowing you didn't just survive but rather, you chose to become *someone* because of it, then that is the blessing, the empowerment that is your birthright.

That choice and your commitment to it, is the most powerful thing you will ever do, not only for you, but for the world around you. There will be a sense that your survival wasn't random and that, maybe, something inside you is ready to create, to contribute, to become.

And then, almost immediately, something else shows up.

Resistance.

That's how it was for me at least. The moment I started asking, *"What now?"* I was met with a thousand reasons why I shouldn't try. My mind offered these reasons up on a silver platter and invited me to sit down at the Table of Excuses for a lavish pity party.

Who do you think you are?

No one cares what you have to say!

Your children are too small, what kind of mother needs more than their children to feel purposeful?

Nothing you have to say is going to help anyone.

Everyone is going to think you are all about yourself.

It's going to be too much work.

And on and on and on the guests at the table would continue to sit down, until I felt physically ill.

But then, after a while. I got so tired and sick of being in the same damn place year after year that I decided not to listen anymore. I knew I was here to do something more than to stay exactly where I was—safe, silent, and slowly shrinking into the horizon of what was left of my life.

Here's the truth (and it's a hard one!): Most people don't fail to find their purpose because they don't have one—they fail because something gets in the way of *committing* to it. And that something, is usually themselves.

We don't talk enough about the way fear shape-shifts and how trauma lingers long after the event. It's hard to define, but oftentimes stepping into something new can feel even scarier than what nearly broke us, but eventually, the pain of staying stuck becomes too painful and we are forced to make those choices. But think about all that wasted time spent at the Table of Excuses with all the things that hold us back!

So let's name them.

Let's name what holds us back—because that's the first step in releasing its power.

Oh, **shame**. The emotion that makes us believe we're too broken to be of use anymore. We think purpose is reserved for people who have it all together—people who didn't lose years to grief, or rage, or just getting by. Shame takes over our brains so that we forget that it's *the cracks that let the light through.*

And then, there is the terror of **being seen**, especially in the aftermath of trauma. When you've been exposed before—emotionally, physically, spiritually—you build walls in order to protect yourself. Purpose, by nature, asks you to come out from behind those walls and expose yourself in all sorts of ways for the greater good. It can feel threatening, even when the danger is long gone, and it takes a while to work up our courage. But don't forget that you did not survive in order to fade into the background. Unless you want to, of course, and that is okay too. At least for a while.

Some of us feel like **frauds**. We tell ourselves we haven't healed enough. That we need one more credential, one more breakthrough, one more clean ending before we can step forward and offer something to the world. But healing doesn't make you useful. *Honesty* does. I know. Mic drop.

Some of us feel **guilty for wanting more**. This was a big one for me. I had the most elite special operations unit in the developed world jump out of airplanes, parachute into the desert on a moonless night, hike two miles in and kill my captors as they rescued me and brought me back to life. *What more could I freaking ask for?!* This kept me stuck for a long time. I kept thinking of all the other hostages that never made it, either before a rescue was attempted, or during an operation that went wrong. I couldn't stop thinking about all the people in the world who were still suffering greatly, and now I, of all people, was dreaming of joy? I wanted more?

So I could build something beautiful? *How dare I???*

But guess what? There is not a quota of good or bad that happens to us. We don't get nine miracles in life and then we are not entitled to ask for more. Life just doesn't work that way. Yes. *You are allowed.* Your thriving does not take anything from anyone else. In fact, it gives permission for others to stop accepting breadcrumbs from the Table of Excuses and puts them in charge of creating their own perfect meal. Life is a feast and it should be consumed to fill us up to overflowing. Regardless of what we have been through or from where we have come.

Some of us are still clinging to the person we were **before**. We can't stop thinking about the one with the life we lost. We ruminate over the job, the calling, the relationships that made sense. We think that if we commit to something new, we're letting go of the past, and if we let go of the past, we'll be saying goodbye forever to the person that is gone, the experiences that we had or the person we were then.

But we're not betraying it or them, rather, we're *honoring* all that was, by continuing to live.

But mostly, I think some of us are just so damn **tired**. The kind of tired that doesn't go away with sleep because it's the kind that comes from carrying grief in your bones, and when all you can really picture is just crawling into bed and never moving, purpose feels like a mountain to climb when you're still just trying to breathe. But purpose doesn't ask you to sprint up that mountain. It just asks you to move, one step at a time. Even if it just starts with your big toe.

Some of us believe that if it's not **big**, it doesn't count. We think purpose needs to be loud, visible, and marketable. But the truth is, some of the most sacred-purpose work happens in private. It happens in kitchens, scratched in the wee hours of the morning in our journals, through the whispered "I love you's" in our children's hair after they have fallen asleep.

If any of these things are holding you back, I want you to hear this:

You are not wrong. You are not broken. You are not behind.

You are human.

And naming what's holding you back is not a sign of weakness—it's a sign that you're almost ready to commit and move; that you are almost ready to rise. You don't have to be fearless or have it all figured out. You just have to be willing to ask: *What if I stopped letting this fear decide who I'm allowed to become?*

Because that's where surviving survival becomes something more. That's where your next chapter begins.

Survivor Spotlight: Danielle's Story— A Promise in the Dark

Danielle was seventeen when she survived the worst night of her life.

It was 1979 in Oregon when she was raped by a man who would later be known as the Jogger Rapist, Richard Gillmore—who would go on to admit to assaulting at least nine women. As he attacked her, he told her he was going to kill her. Danielle wanted to fight, but more than anything, she wanted to live. As she was being attacked, her mother's words came back to her mind when in passing one day, she had once given Danielle a piece of advice no daughter should ever need: *If something like that ever happens, don't resist. Just survive.*

And that's what she did.

After the assault, Danielle called the police, and she was taken to the hospital, where she underwent a rape kit and an invasive police interview. She was lucky, in a way—they believed her. But that didn't mean she felt safe.

She went home, stepped into the shower, and tried to scrub the experience off her skin—she couldn't scrub hard enough. Then, she crawled into bed and sobbed. Everything she had imagined for her life—marriage, family, the fairytale she'd always dreamed of—felt gone, it had disappeared into a violent puff of dust.

That night, in that dark place, Danielle felt so hollowed out and empty. All she knew to do was pray, "God, if you help me survive this, I promise I'll help other rape victims someday."

And then—she buried it.

Danielle didn't tell anyone about the violent attack except one person: the man who would become her husband. He showed up at her door one day, guitar in hand, for a church group meeting and she knew he was the one. When she told him her story, she expected rejection, and fell even deeper for him when instead, he gave her love, safety, and thirty years of unwavering support.

As a means of survival, Danielle poured herself into mother-hood; she built a family, a business—she created a life that looked full from the outside, but inside, she was still living in fear.

She couldn't be home alone at night, she had PTSD before she had the words to name it.

Because she was so desperate to escape what had happened, she erased her rapist's name from her memory and locked that chapter away, convinced that forgetting was the only way forward.

Seven years passed, then one day, in 1986, she got a call. Richard Gillmore had been caught—thanks in part to the composite sketch she'd helped police create back in 1979.

Danielle was shocked to learn that there were at least eight other victims, but because of Oregon's three-year statute of limitations, he could only be charged with one rape and it wasn't hers.

Still, she stayed quiet. More than twenty years passed and then, another call came.

It was the Multnomah County District Attorney's office letting her know Gillmore was up for parole and they were asking Danielle to testify. She was shocked to be confronted with this secret she had kept under lock and key for so long.

So she said no. She tried to explain that she didn't want to be "the rape victim" and that she didn't feel she had the strength to dig that pain up again. She thought she had put it behind her.

But then she turned on the news and saw another survivor sharing her story, the one whose case was not under the statute of limitations, and something inside her shifted.

The promise she made as a teenager—the one she prayed through tears and shock and blood—rose to the surface and came back to her memory. She knew she had made a mistake and needed to rectify it. The next day, she called the prosecutor back. "I made the wrong decision," she told him. "Whatever you need me to do, I'll do it."

A week later, she was asked to share her story with *The Oregonian* and that terrified her. Reading her old police report sent her spiraling; she had never been able to read it before. She was struck with how naive and young she sounded, and once again was reminded of the innocence that had been stolen so violently from her. Gathering her courage and asking God for strength, she stepped forward anyway—and when she did, something unexpected happened.

The other survivors began coming forward too. One voice gave rise to many and what became heartbreakingly clear was this: Richard Gillmore hadn't just sentenced his victims to one violent act. He had sentenced them to lives of fear, silence, and shame. He wasn't the only one who had been handed a life sentence.

Danielle decided that if she couldn't get justice retroactively, she could fight for others to have it going forward and so she began to show up at parole hearings and made efforts to start changing laws. She stood in the same room as the man who tried to kill her and realized something incredible: "I wasn't afraid of him anymore," she said. "He didn't count on me using my voice."

Even then, because of the expired statute of limitations, she wasn't legally allowed to testify at one parole hearing—so she fought to change the law.

In 2009, Oregon eliminated the statute of limitations in cases where DNA evidence is present.

In 2012, she filed a state lawsuit through the National Crime Victim Law Institute so that she could testify and keep this man behind bars. Three years later, she helped pass legislation allowing any survivor to speak at a parole hearing, regardless of whether they were serving time for that specific crime. In 2015, she extended the statute of limitations on rape for cases outside of DNA evidence from six years to twelve in the state of Oregon.

To date, Danielle has now played a key role in passing ten bills in Oregon and eight in Oklahoma, where she now lives, and she is only getting started. She is contemplating running for office, and is currently working as the Attorney General's designee to the Sexual Assault Forensic Evidence Board. She chairs the subcommittee on recommendations and evaluations. Working closely with the board, she continues to effect real change so that she can continue making a difference for the women who continue to be violently assaulted and their perpetrators are not convicted of their crimes. She has worked with the Joyful Heart Foundation on rape kit reform and has become a trusted advocate, not because she had credentials—but because she had lived it.

"At first, I saw myself as a wounded woman. But then I looked around at the community that had formed—and I saw a lion," Danielle says about herself. During our interview she told me she often doesn't recognize the woman she has become—but she likes her. "I have more to offer the world than just my sad story," she told me. She has *strength* to offer. She has passion and resolve and the will to make things easier for the women who continue to suffer at the hands of these violent criminals.

"Danielle is a go-getter. She does whatever it takes to make things happen," said Ilse Knecht, director of policy and advocacy for Joyful Heart Foundation in New York. "She is fairly unique. She's made that bridge from survivor to advocate and now activist, all three of those things in one person."

Danielle credits the incredible support she has garnered from the district attorney's office, attorney general's office, the governor's office, law enforcement, crime victim advocates, as well as various legislators that have offered her a seat at the table of changemakers. She admits that she wouldn't be where she is right now if it weren't for the people that God has put along her path, all along the way. From the policemen that believed her the night of her assault, to the other victims that have come around her to offer support, Danielle knows she is not alone.

She reminds survivors: "You don't need a fancy degree or a lot of money to make a change. You just need the right people around you—and the fire to keep going."

How Danielle's Story Reflects the RISE Framework

Danielle's story is not one of quick healing or simple justice. It is the story of a woman who lived under the weight of violent trauma for decades—until the promise she made to survive became the mission that transformed her life and the laws that failed her.

R - Reckon with the Pain

Danielle didn't get to process what happened right away. At seventeen, she did what she needed to do to stay alive—and then she buried it. For decades, she lived with the silent, persistent symptoms of PTSD: fear, hypervigilance, shame. She didn't speak about the rape. She couldn't even say her perpetrator's name. But when she was asked to testify decades later, she came face-to-face with the trauma she thought she had outrun. She didn't just remember—she relived.

And still, she said yes.

I – Identify the Impact

Danielle believed for years that she had moved on. She had a good marriage, children, and a business she built with her own hands. But the truth was still there, etched in her bones.

She couldn't be home alone at night. She lived with unspoken terror. Only when the legal system came calling did she begin to realize: this never left me. And she made a different choice—not to push it down, but to speak it out loud.

S – Seek the Meaning

Danielle didn't look for meaning in what happened to her. There was no silver lining in violence. But she did find meaning in what she did with it. The promise she made at seventeen—to help other rape victims if she survived—became her North Star. Her healing began the moment she remembered that vow and chose to keep it. Speaking out wasn't just for herself.

It was so other women could speak too. So victims wouldn't keep carrying life sentences in silence.

E – Embody the Purpose

Danielle has changed laws. She's spoken at legislative hearings, testified at parole board hearings, and stood in rooms she was once too afraid to enter. She's been an active participant in passing *eighteen pieces of legislation* between Oregon and Oklahoma. She has worked with the Joyful Heart Foundation, served on task forces, work groups, and helped clear rape kit backlogs. She funds her own travel to continue this work—because she believes in it that much. She reminds us that you don't need power to make change. You need truth. You need grit. And you need a promise you're not afraid to keep.

PAUSE, PONDER, AND PROCESS

Let these questions help you listen to the quiet resistance within—and choose to move forward anyway.

1. **What is the story I'm telling myself about why I can't step into my purpose yet?**
   Where did that story come from?
   Is it still true?

2. **Do I believe I have to be fully healed before I'm allowed to help others or contribute something meaningful?**
   What if healing and purpose could happen side by side?

3. **Where do I still feel unsafe being seen, known, or heard?**
   What part of me is trying to protect me by staying small?

4. **Have I ever felt guilty for dreaming about joy or impact after my survival?**
   What would it look like to honor my pain *and* make space for desire?

5. **Am I holding on to a version of myself that no longer fits—because it feels safer than stepping into someone new?**

6. **What fear would I have to face if I fully committed to the thing that's calling me?**

7. **What does "purpose" look like right now—in this season, with what I have?**
   What's one small, low-pressure way I can begin to commit?

RISE Reminders: What You Name, You Can Release

Come back to these truths when your fear tells you it's safer not to try.

- I don't have to wait to be ready. I just have to be willing.
- There is no perfect time to begin—only the time I choose to stop waiting.
- My resistance is not a sign to quit. It's a sign that I'm close to something that matters.
- Letting go of who I was makes space for who I'm becoming.
- It's not selfish to want more from life. It's sacred.
- My healing doesn't have to be complete to be meaningful.
- I don't have to be fearless to take the next step. I just have to move with the fear.

CHAPTER 13
THE OVERFLOW

Turning Survival into Shared Abundance

We often imagine survival as a solitary victory—pulling ourselves through impossible terrain, inch by inch, toward some future where the pain no longer dictates the terms. And for a while, that might be enough. But eventually, if we're lucky—and if we're brave—we begin to see that survival isn't the final destination. It's the door.

But what is on the other side of that door? Our fear and resistance would have us believe it is a scary monster of failure and epic humiliation (or is that just me???). But I would like to present you with a reframe: perhaps there is opportunity waiting for you on the other side of your surviving survival threshold. Not just for yourself, but for those who are still in the wilderness you once walked through.

My friend and mentor Krista Clive-Smith, whom you met earlier, always asks me to consider the three following questions: What life do you want to lead? Who do you want to serve? and What business do you want to be in? She also blew my mind when (within the context of business) she shared the insight that my ideal client is a past version of myself. For the purposes of purpose, I would say, the ideal person to serve would be the past version of yourself. Who did you need to show up for you when you were in the throes of surviving survival? I needed someone who would help lead me to information that would get me here—but I couldn't find anyone, no matter how hard I tried. My prayer and greatest hope is that this book will serve you in that way. I want to be the person for you that I so badly needed when I was desperate in my surviving survival phase.

One of the most radical shifts in a survivor's life is the transition from scarcity to stewardship. Scarcity says: *There's only enough for me.* Stewardship says: *Because I made it, I can make a way for you.*

Creating opportunity—real, soul-nourishing abundance—for others is the sacred work of someone who has survived and *chosen* to become a source. That doesn't mean you have everything figured out. It means you've walked through something hard and come out with tools in your hands, and now you ask, *Who else could use these?*

It means your pain didn't just shape you—it equipped you. And your healing is no longer just personal. It's catalytic.

Survivor Spotlight: Rebecca Bender—From Surviving to System-Changing

Rebecca Bender is a fierce, living example of this kind of stewardship. A survivor of human trafficking, she spent six years trapped in a world most of us only hear about on the news. Her trafficker lured her with false promises of love and safety, but what followed was coercion, violence, and exploitation.

Eventually, through determination and a mother who never gave up, Rebecca escaped.

But what's remarkable isn't just her survival—it's what she *did* with it.

Rather than stay silent or hide, Rebecca chose to speak. She wrote her memoir, *In Pursuit of Love: One Woman's Journey from Trafficked to Triumphant*, to help others understand the manipulative nature of trafficking and how someone could be both victim and fighter at the same time. She founded the **Rebecca Bender Initiative** (RBI), which now trains law enforcement, service providers, and corporations across the country on how to identify and support trafficking survivors.

Even more, she created **Elevate Academy**—an online school created specifically for survivors to gain leadership skills, build careers, and reclaim their voices in spaces they were once shut out of.

Through her nonprofit and her survivor-centered Elevate Academy, she has helped nearly 1,700 women in twenty-two countries reclaim their futures through professional development, leadership training, and trauma-informed support. Rebecca has personally trained more than 143,000 professionals—from FBI agents to frontline responders—on how to investigate, identify, and support trafficking survivors, bringing a human-centered lens to systems that once overlooked them. In 2022 alone, RBI provided over 3,600 hours of free education to survivors, and within a year of completing Elevate Academy, 95 percent of participants reported increased income, with 90 percent gaining employability skills that shifted their economic trajectory. Rebecca didn't just escape the world that once trapped her—she went back with a lantern and lit the path for thousands more to rise.

Her story is a blueprint of what it looks like to turn trauma into transformation, and transformation into *infrastructure* for others to rise.

How Rebecca's Story Reflects the RISE Framework

Rebecca Bender's life is a powerful example of what it means to survive survival—and then to turn that survival into meaningful contribution for others.

After escaping nearly six years of human trafficking, Rebecca didn't simply move on and leave the past behind.

She faced it. She allowed it to shape her—not into someone diminished, but into someone who would change systems, communities, and lives.

Her story beautifully mirrors the stages of the RISE framework.

R – Reckon with the Pain

Rebecca had to face the deep wounds left by her exploitation. The trauma didn't disappear once she escaped. She had to confront the shame, the grief, the identity loss that followed, rather than pretending she could just "move forward." Reckoning with her pain was the first step in reclaiming her story.

I – Identify the Impact

Rather than suppress what had happened, Rebecca allowed herself to see how deeply it had shaped her life—her beliefs, her relationships, her sense of self-worth.

She didn't minimize the impact, but rather, she named it, studied it, and began to understand it.

Only by acknowledging the depth of the wound could she begin to build something new.

S – Seek the Meaning

Instead of letting her trauma be a period at the end of her story, Rebecca looked for what she could create from it. She turned her experience into a calling—founding the Rebecca Bender Initiative and launching Elevate Academy to equip and empower survivors around the world.

She sought meaning by ensuring that what she endured could light a path for others to find freedom and dignity.

E – Embody the Purpose

Today, Rebecca's legacy reaches far beyond her personal survival. Through her training programs, her memoir *In Pursuit of Love*, and her leadership in survivor advocacy, she continues to build bridges for others. Her life is proof that surviving survival isn't the end—it's the beginning of a ripple effect that can change systems, shift narratives, and save lives.

Rebecca's journey shows us that thriving doesn't mean forgetting what happened. It means refusing to let it be the only thing that defines you. It means building a life—and a legacy—that transforms hardship into hope for others.

* * *

You don't have to be a founder, a public speaker, or someone with a massive platform to create a ripple effect. Some of the most life-changing acts of abundance happen in the margins—unseen, uncelebrated, but no less powerful.

It can be as simple as making space for someone else's voice at the table, especially when you know what it feels like to be unheard.

It's listening deeply, then stepping back to let someone else step forward. It's helping a friend believe in their next chapter when they can't yet see past the last one. Sometimes it's sharing a resource, a name, or a number—something that seems small to you but could quietly change the trajectory of someone else's life.

It might look like mentoring someone into the kind of life you once only dreamed of, or offering your own story not as a spotlight, but as a lighthouse—steady and lit, simply to say, "You're not alone out here."

Abundance, in this light, is not about having more. It's about *moving* more—circulating the healing, wisdom, and access we've gained so others can experience their own rising. It's less about what you've acquired and more about what you're willing to pass on.

True abundance is never about accumulation. It's about **liberation**—for you, and for the people who get to walk through the doors you once had to kick down alone.

The New Definition of Purpose

What if purpose isn't found in accolades, but in overflow? What if you measured your impact not in followers, dollars, or stages—but in the number of people who now believe something is possible because *you* believed it first?

When we start living this way, we realize: The trauma that once threatened to define us becomes the soil from which *legacy* grows. Rebecca says it this way: "Your past doesn't disqualify you—it prepares you."

And when you use that preparation to lift others, to empower, to mentor, to teach—you've stepped into a kind of purpose that no hardship can take away.

There was a time when I believed that survival would be the end of the story—that making it home, breathing air that wasn't filled with fear, would somehow be enough for me to move on. And in the beginning, it was. Survival was a victory. Survival was sacred. But eventually, I realized that survival alone wasn't the destination. It was the starting point.

My captivity taught me about endurance, about fear, about surrender. But surviving survival—*learning to live after living through the unthinkable*—taught me something even deeper: that my pain could either remain a closed chapter or it could become a doorway for others. And so, I made a choice: I chose to believe that the trauma meant for my destruction could be turned into a force for abundance—not just for myself, but for the people whose paths I would cross. I chose to build something with the very hands that once trembled. I chose to create opportunity, to offer hope, to be a lighthouse when all I had once seen was darkness.

I turned my life's hardest moment into something meaningful by refusing to hoard my healing. I wrote my story not just to be heard, but to make someone else feel less alone. I built retreats, courses, and safe spaces not because I had all the answers, but because I knew what it felt like to wander without a map. I spoke, not to relive my suffering, but to remind others that rising is possible—that rising is already happening inside them, even when it feels invisible.

Abundance, I've learned, isn't about accumulation or applause. It's about *circulation*. It's about letting the wisdom, resilience, and hope you fought so hard to gather move freely through you and into the lives of others.

If my survival can open even one door for someone else—if it can create even one flicker of possibility in a heart that feels trapped—then it hasn't just been survival.

It's been **multiplication**. It's been **meaning**. It's been **legacy**.

And that is the most abundant life I can imagine living.

PAUSE, PONDER, AND PROCESS

1. **Who has inspired you by turning their survival into something bigger than themselves?**

2. **What parts of your journey are equipped to become someone else's lifeline?**

3. **Where are you already practicing abundance in small, quiet ways?**

4. **If you created something—a program, a letter, a space, a story—for others walking through what you once did, what would it look like?**

5. **What would it mean to *become* the opportunity you once needed?**

6. **Write about someone you've helped simply because of who you've become.**
   What did you offer? What did they receive? How did that moment impact you both?

7. **Imagine your life as a bridge.**
   What's on the other side of that bridge? Who's crossing it because of the path you've made?

RISE Reminders

- I honor the truth of what I've been through, knowing it has shaped me—but it doesn't have to limit me.
- My pain can become a path, not a prison.
- What I survived has given me insight, empathy, and strength—and I choose to use that to light the way for others.
- I don't have to do something loud to live with purpose. My quiet, intentional offerings are already creating meaning in ways I may never fully see.
- My healing is not just for me—it's a gift I get to pass on. Every time I create space, share my story, or lift someone else, I am building something bigger than survival. I am building legacy.

CHAPTER 14
IT'S TIME TO THRIVE

Thriving doesn't mean your life has gone according to plan. Sometimes, it's exactly the opposite.

Sometimes thriving begins when the plan falls apart, and you choose to keep moving forward anyway.

Survivor's Spotlight: Pachion Moore—More than Just a Statistic

My friend Pachion Moore knows this firsthand. At seventeen years old, Pachion had her whole future mapped out. She was active on her high school cheerleading squad, a student leader, and deeply involved in her school community. Her dreams were big, and they felt within reach.

And then everything changed when she found out she was pregnant. She says it felt like the life she had been building came crashing down overnight. The father wanted nothing to do with her and the world around her offered quick judgment and low expectations. Statistically, people expected her story to end there.

But, Pachion made a decision—one that would alter the entire trajectory of her life: She chose not to become a statistic. It was the hardest thing she has ever done, but she chose to thrive.

Pachion is incredibly smart and she used her resourceful skill-set to find local resources that could support her as a young single mother. She moved back home so she could continue her dream of going to college, and while studying for her degree with a baby by her side wasn't exactly how she had envisioned her college experience, she kept pressing on because she knew she and her baby boy were worth working for.

Today, Pachion is a certified life coach with an extensive background in working with nonprofits who support young women in crisis. She is the founder of **NewMOMents**, an organization dedicated to empowering young single mothers through job shadowing, life skills training, career development, and personalized coaching. Her organization helps young women build secure, fulfilling futures for themselves and their children, and their mission is very clear: They want to inspire confidence, empower resilience, and create lasting change in order to break down barriers and create real pathways to success for young mothers who refuse to be defined by their hardest moments.

Pachion's story is a living example that thriving isn't about everything going perfectly.

It's about choosing to grow even when the odds are against you and refusing to let your lowest moment be the final word. Pachion has shown herself, her son, and the world around her that you can build a beautiful life not just in spite of hardship, but *because you believe you are capable of so much more.*

Her belief that there are no mistakes, just lessons to be learned, is one of the keys to surviving survival. She models beautifully that we can overcome the most impossible odds, if we just continue to believe that we are worthy of it and let it take the time it needs to take.

More than anything though, Pachion shows us that thriving is a choice we get to make—not once, but over and over again.

How Pachion's Story Reflects the RISE Framework
R – Reckon with the Pain

Pachion faced the reality that her life had changed dramatically when she found out she was pregnant.

Instead of denying it, running from it, or pretending it wasn't happening, she reckoned honestly with her situation. She accepted that her old dreams might have to look different—and that she would need to find new strength to move forward.

I – Identify the Impact

She recognized the profound impact her pregnancy had—not just on her future plans, but on her identity, her relationships, and how others perceived her. Instead of letting society's low expectations define her, she identified what mattered most to her: finishing her education, providing a better life for her child, and believing in her own worth.

S – Seek the Meaning

Pachion didn't just work through her situation—she made meaning from it. She decided that her experience could be fuel for something bigger. By starting NewMOMents, she took what was once her hardest chapter and transformed it into a mission to help other young mothers believe in themselves and create lasting change.

E – Embody the Purpose

Through NewMOMents, Pachion extends her healing outward. She's not just thriving for herself; she's opening doors, building community, and creating a ripple effect of resilience for young women who might otherwise believe their story has already been written.

I can't point to a single moment when I knew it was time to thrive. It didn't come with a grand epiphany or a dramatic turning point. For me, it was quieter than that. The exact opposite of the tsunami that ripped my life in two all those years ago, the rebuilding happened with such minutiae that I didn't even notice that before long, I had reinvented a life that I felt was worth something.

It felt like a gradual unfolding, the way seasons shift—almost unnoticeable at first, until suddenly you realize the air has changed and all the colors in the sky, the leaves on the trees—everything is so much more vivid in the way it shows up in the world than you remember it ever being before.

For a long time, surviving was the right focus. It took all the energy I had just to get through the day, to steady my footing after everything that had been shaken loose. Survival was necessary and sacred. But over time, I began to notice small things, little shifts. Moments when I laughed without having to force it, or those spaces of time where the anxiety let up off my chest and I realized I could just . . . breathe. Then, there came the times when I felt curious again. It was a familiar feeling I thought I had lost, wondering what might be possible with the days that loomed in front of me, instead of assuming nothing of interest ever would be. I started to have ideas, and dream up projects that made me feel a little more alive, rather than weighed down with all the work and possibility of failure.

There wasn't a rush to move forward, but there was a growing sense that simply surviving wasn't enough anymore—not because I was ungrateful, but because I had more life inside me than surviving survival could contain.

I realized I didn't want to live in constant reaction to my past—I wanted to build something new.

I was ready to explore what else might be possible. But it wasn't loud or urgent.

It was just time.

* * *

There's a difference between surviving and thriving. This may seem obvious, but the reality is, a whole lot of people continue managing their survival under the impression that they are thriving.

After living through something hard—whether it's trauma, loss, illness, or another life-altering event—**survival itself can feel like thriving** for a while, and in many ways, it is.

When you've known the feeling of barely making it through a day, any sense of stability or forward movement can feel like a huge victory. And I want to be very clear: it is a victory. But sometimes, we mistake the *absence of immediate crisis* for thriving. We think because we aren't falling apart anymore, we must be flourishing or because life looks "normal" on the outside, we must be healed on the inside. The truth is, **survival and thriving can look very similar from the outside**—routine, productivity, even success—but the *inner experience* tells a different story.

The tricky thing about surviving survival is that it can start to feel so normal, we hardly realize we're still doing it. When we're still in survival mode, we often make decisions from a place of fear or scarcity without even realizing it. We might say yes to things that don't align with us because we're afraid of losing connection. We might stay silent about what we really need because speaking up still feels risky. Even when everything around us seems fine, we carry a kind of invisible exhaustion—the kind that no amount of sleep seems to fix.

We might find it hard to trust good things when they come, always bracing ourselves for the moment they might be taken away. Or, we find ourselves staying busy, sometimes overwhelmingly so, filling our schedules and our lives not because we feel free, but because somewhere inside, we're still trying to stay one step ahead of vulnerability.

Joy feels fleeting. Rest feels suspicious. Dreams feel dangerous.

But when we begin to move into thriving, something shifts. We start making choices based on what we actually desire, not just what feels safe. We make decisions that align with our values and our vision, not just our fears. We begin to feel more grounded, even when challenges arise, because our sense of safety comes from within, not from controlling every variable around us. We learn to trust ourselves—and to trust life a little more—to hold the good things, without constantly scanning for loss or disappointment. We allow ourselves to connect, to rest, to celebrate small victories without guilt. Joy feels real again. Growth feels not just possible, but welcome. And the future doesn't feel like something we have to defend ourselves against—it starts to feel like a place of possibility, of expansion, of hope.

Thriving doesn't mean everything is easy or perfect, it simply means we are living with more openness than fear, more intention than reaction, more creation than survival. It's not something that happens all at once.

It's something we choose, a little more, every day.

If we believe we're thriving when we're actually still surviving, we might unknowingly limit ourselves—we might stop growing too soon and settle for "good enough" when life is quietly waiting, wanting to offer us *so much more.*

Recognizing that we're still surviving in some ways isn't a failure. It's an invitation—to be curious, to be compassionate with ourselves, and to gently ask: *What else might be possible for me?* True thriving isn't about doing more but about *being more fully who we are*—unarmored, unhurried, and unapologetically alive.

Surviving survival is about holding on through the hardest moments after we have survived the trauma, it's about endurance, protection, and staying afloat after the storm has wreaked its havoc on us. For a long time, surviving that is enough—and it should be. *It's sacred work to stay alive when life has asked the unthinkable of you.* And then some.

Thriving doesn't erase what happened though, it simply refuses to let what happened be the limit of what's possible next. It may not feel like it now, but it is possible to be in a space where you are beyond living in constant reaction to fear, loss, or survival instincts.

You *will* plant roots down again, you *will* grow deliberately, and you *can* live with intention—not just in a state of high alert, proceeding with caution. I promise.

As we've discussed, thriving takes work. It looks like investing your energy into relationships, creativity, purpose, and joy. It looks like making choices not just to stay safe, but to become fully, freely alive. It's allowing yourself to imagine a future that's bigger than just getting by.

It's believing that you're allowed to build a life that feels good, not just one that feels bearable.

Thriving is quiet sometimes and often unseen by the world, but you can feel it, can't you? You can feel it in your body, your mind, your spirit. It's the moment you realize you're no longer simply existing—but rather, you're living from a place of hope, curiosity, and deep resilience.

And it's time. Not later. Not someday. Now.

When We Thrive, We Give Others Permission Too

There's something powerful about watching someone move into thriving because it reminds us that it's possible. It gives others quiet permission to believe they can thrive too, even if their timeline looks different. This is why I tell my story. This is why I started my publishing company. This is why I am active on social media—I desperately want other people to know it is possible to thrive.

You have to choose to understand that deciding to thrive doesn't erase what you've been through.

It honors it by saying, *What I endured shaped me, but it does not define my limits.*

Your thriving becomes part of the legacy you leave behind—an example of resilience lived out, not just endured.

PAUSE, PONDER, AND PROCESS

1. **In what ways have you already moved beyond survival, even if you haven't named it yet?**

2. **What parts of your life feel ready for growth, not just maintenance?**

3. **What does thriving mean to you personally— not what it looks like for others?**

4. **How can you give yourself permission to experience more joy and expansion, without guilt?**

RISE Reminders

- I honor my story, but I'm not bound by it. I am free to keep growing.
- My experiences have strengthened my roots and expanded my reach.
- Thriving is not forgetting what happened. It's choosing to live fully because of what I've learned.
- When I thrive, I show others that healing doesn't have to end in survival—it can blossom into something even more.

CONCLUSION

When I set out to write this book, I knew from the beginning that it wasn't just about surviving trauma. It was always going to be about something deeper—something most people don't talk about. It was going to be about *surviving survival itself.*

I knew firsthand that the hardest part isn't always the moment of crisis. Sometimes, it's the long, quiet work that comes after—the work of putting your life, your identity, and your heart back together again. The work of figuring out how to live *after* you've lived through the unimaginable.

But what I didn't realize when I began writing was just how much more I would come to understand about my own journey in surviving survival. Writing this book made me confront the parts of my healing I hadn't fully named. It made me see that survival isn't just about enduring what happens to you. It's about choosing, again and again, who you want to become afterward.

It's about grieving what was lost—and still believing in what's possible. It's about holding space for pain and hope at the same time. It's about learning to live in a way that isn't ruled by fear, but rooted in purpose, connection, and quiet courage.

In these pages, we've walked through that deeper landscape together. You've honored your survival—and you've dared to imagine what life could look like beyond it.

You've reckoned with the impact of what you've been through. You've searched for meaning in places you once thought were only broken. You've allowed yourself to consider that you are meant for more than just getting by. And maybe, most importantly, you've begun to see that thriving isn't a reward you have to earn. It's a way of being that grows naturally from everything you've already survived, learned, and built.

If there's one thing I hope you carry forward, it's this:

You are not just someone who made it through something hard. You are someone who has survived survival itself.

That kind of strength cannot be undone. You don't owe the world your suffering.

You don't have to keep proving your worthiness. You are allowed to live with fullness, with joy, with purpose—because you are here, and because your life matters.

Healing isn't a straight line, therefore thriving isn't a finish line.

But every day you choose hope, growth, connection, and creation—you are living proof that surviving survival is possible. And that beautiful things can grow from even the hardest ground.

Your next chapter isn't about erasing what happened. It's about building something meaningful because of everything you now know.

And you are ready. You always have been.

A BLESSING FOR
YOUR NEXT CHAPTER...

To the one who has walked through fire and still dares to hope—this blessing is for you.

May you know, deep in your bones, that you are more than what you have survived.
You are more than the losses, the battles, the nights you thought would break you.
You are the one who stayed. The one who chose life, even when it asked more of you than you thought you could give.
May you never again mistake endurance for your only gift. You are not here just to get through.
You are here to build, to create, to expand into the full, radiant story of who you are becoming.
May the days ahead bring not just healing, but *wholeness*.
Not just survival, but *joy*.
Not just closure, but *new beginnings*.
May you find people who see you clearly—and may you let them.

May you trust the sound of your own voice, the strength of your
own hands, the wisdom of your own heart.
And may you trust that the life you are building—imperfect,
beautiful, still unfolding—is already enough.
You are not late to your life.
You are right on time.
Your next chapter is not an afterthought.
It is a masterpiece in progress.
May you walk forward with courage, with tenderness,
and with the steady knowing that you were always meant
for more than survival.